REYNOLDS REMEMBERS

20 Years with the Sacramento Kings

Jerry Reynolds with Don Drysdale

Foreword by Grant Napear

www.SportsPublishingLLC.com

ISBN: 1-59670-137-4

Publishers: Peter L. Bannon and Joseph J. Bannon Sr.
Senior managing editor: Susan M. Moyer
Acquisitions editor: Mike Pearson
Developmental editor: Travis W. Moran
Art director: K. Jeffrey Higgerson
Dust jacket design: Dustin J. Hubbart
Interior layout: Dustin J. Hubbart
Imaging: Dustin J. Hubbart
Photo editor: Erin Linden-Levy
Media and promotions managers: Randy Fouts (national), Maurey Williamson (print)

Printed in the United States of America

Sports Publishing L.L.C.
804 North Neil Street
Champaign, IL 61820

Phone: 1-877-424-2665
Fax: 217-363-2073
www.SportsPublishingLLC.com

He never drained a game-winning jumper, cleared a rebound, led a fast break, or swatted away a shot, but Bill Jones did just about everything else for 23 seasons as the team's trainer. "Jonesy," as he was affectionately known, died last year of cancer at the age of 69.

Jonesy retired in 1995, before playoff shares became a given for the team's staff. His job description was simple: Keep the players healthy, because there's always another game. While he never ran onto the court to a standing ovation with fireworks blasting and rock music blaring, his importance to the team went far beyond making sure that the ankles were taped.

These days, the Kings and every other NBA team fly from city to city in chartered planes. But when the Kings first came to Sacramento, they flew commercial. Jonesy was not only the trainer, but also the traveling secretary.

In the franchise's bad old days, it was left to Jonesy—with his easygoing manner, quick smile, wit, and large stack of greenbacks—to smooth things over with hoteliers and bus companies who were leery of the sometimes slow-to-pay Kings. When a group of players pulled a dine-and-dash at a Denny's in Cleveland, Jonesy quietly convinced the manager not to press charges when the cops showed up in the lobby of the team's hotel. Jonesy took care of all the details, whether it was loading luggage or finding a practice facility on the road. He did a thankless and difficult job with good cheer, grace, and dignity.

Beyond that, Jonesy was a father confessor for players and the confidant of coaches. He had a kind word and a joke for everybody—the kind of guy you'd want as your neighbor or fishing buddy. Many players turned to Jonesy when they were disappointed in their playing time, experienced self-doubt, or had personal problems. Coaches knew that they could count on Jonesy to listen patiently when they had to rant and counted on his insight into the physical and mental state of the players.

Jonesy even had the grace to befriend the league's pariahs—referees and sports writers. One longtime Kings beat writer, in particular, is grateful that Jonesy managed more than once to stall the team bus long enough for a story to be filed on deadline.

Jonesy's insight into human nature was so uncanny that the Kings had an unwritten law known simply as "The Jonesy Rule": If someone new in the organization couldn't get along with Jonesy, their character was considered suspect. Jonesy did so much for this franchise that it doesn't seem right to ask anything more of him. But here's one last request:

Jonesy ... if the Kings are playing the Lakers in the playoffs, and the free throws aren't dropping, please feel free to provide some divine guidance.

CONTENTS

ACKNOWLEDGMENTS

Remembering 20 seasons with the Sacramento Kings was made much easier with the help and assistance of several people.

The team's Public Relations staff, led by Troy Hanson and assisted by Darrin May, Devin Blankenship, and Chris Clark, went above the call of duty. Also, members of the Basketball Operations department who were extremely helpful included Darryl Arata, Dayna Simondi, and Steve Shuman. Certainly Danette Leighton, Vice President of Marketing, deserves special props for great advice and assistance.

Most importantly this book would have little significance without the outstanding leadership provided by Joe and Gavin Maloof, truly top-of-the-line owners, who provide not only a class basketball team but also a great organization and working environment.

The final credit must go to my family. Without support from Dodie, Jay, and Danielle, this book and my career would have questionable value!

FOREWORD

by Grant Napear

It's hard to imagine the Sacramento Kings without Jerry Reynolds—not that I've ever tried. Jerry and I have worked together on Kings telecasts practically since James Naismith first hung up the peach basket. I've had a blast working with him, and I've learned much from him. Jerry has forgotten more about the NBA than most people know.

Jerry is the only member of the basketball staff who has been with the franchise since it moved from Kansas City in 1985. Being in one place for that long in any business is noteworthy, but doing it in the NBA ... that's saying something. Jerry's ability to roll with the punches over the years is an amazing achievement. He was thrown to the lions a couple of times early in his career, taking over the team after other coaches were fired, and lived to talk about it.

Contrary to some published reports, Jerry isn't made of Teflon. His coaching record is what it is. But where he's stood out—the reason he's a survivor while so many others have come and gone—is the fact that he's not just a character, but has character. Over the years, he has been asked to adjust on the fly, to learn new skills, to swallow his pride, to take the heat: in general, to be the good soldier. He has done all that and more with class and professionalism—and while retaining his sense of humor and a great perspective on life.

Jerry is a big part of Sacramento Kings lore. He saw the original Arco Arena rise from a sheep pasture. He remembers Reggie Theus hunting pheasants in the nearby fields and bringing the birds back to clean them in the locker room. Jerry was on the team's commercial flight that almost went into the Potomac River during a sleet storm. At Arco Arena II, he was on the floor looking up into the rafters the night the roof leaked and the team's original owner, Gregg Lukenbill, climbed onto the catwalk to stop the dripping rather than forfeit the game. Half of Sacramento swears they were there the night Jerry collapsed on the sidelines. Jerry walked out on a news conference without speaking—probably for the first time in his life—after Ricky Berry's suicide. He covered for Bill Russell when Russ didn't want to deal with difficult questions from the media. He made one of the greatest moves in franchise history when he orchestrated the Mitch Richmond trade.

One thing I'll never forget is this past year when the team had its 20th reunion and introduced players from the first season during halftime of a game. Jerry got the loudest applause, and that told me all I needed to know about what Kings fans think of him.

When the Maloof family purchased the Kings seven years ago, everyone in the organization was a little nervous. No one knew whether any, some, or all of the existing staff would be retained. But I never had any doubts that Jerry would be here. Beyond his knowledge of the NBA, he has a tremendous passion for the franchise and the sport (he can't stand it when I talk about hockey), and he's dedicated to his job. Jerry was here through the bad times and deserves as much as anyone to enjoy the good times.

Jerry makes friends and fans wherever he goes. He has represented the team at countless public functions, and I've never seen anyone nod off when he's at the dais. He has a natural ability to relate to casual and hardcore fans alike. I respect the fact that he has taken on whatever challenges have come his way. The Sacramento Monarchs are a good example. Jerry had no knowledge of the women's professional game, but jumped into it, learned, and helped turn the team into a model franchise. Today, his name hangs in the rafters of Arco Arena for his contributions to the Women's National Basketball Association.

When you talk to or hear Jerry for the first time, you can't help but notice his Indiana twang. Because of his accent and the fact that he tends to make fun of himself (and everything else), some people probably think of Jerry as being a hick. Well, he is, but he's a rather sophisticated hick. "I've been to the county fair," he likes to say, "but I've also been to college."

Anyone who's been around Jerry for five minutes has probably heard a story about French Lick or Larry Bird. One time after a shootaround in Indianapolis, we were on the bus waiting for a couple of the guys, and someone asked the bus driver about French

Lick. The driver was an older man, a born-and-bred Hoosier with the same twang as Jerry. Anyway, the driver says, "French Lick—oh yeah, the home of Larry Bird." Then I asked the driver if he had ever heard of Jerry Reynolds. The driver paused for a bit, rubbed his chin with his fingers, and then answered, "No, can't say that I have." You should have heard the bus. Everyone was in stitches because Jerry was sitting right there, and of course, he was laughing as hard as anyone was. The fact that Jerry takes basketball, but not himself, very seriously sets him apart from most people involved in the NBA and television.

The more you listen to Jerry, the more you realize that what he says is honest, considerate, and sensible. Jerry may not be the most handsome color man in the television business, but he's one of the sharpest and wittiest.

I get a kick out of his "Jerry-isms:" a nice play by Mike Bibby becomes "Bib-i-licious;" a couple of consecutive three-pointers by Peja Stojakovic become "Peja Vu;" a blocked shot becomes a "smush;" a nice move to the hoop (or a travel) becomes "a hippity-hop to the barber-shop."

He always cracks me up. You just can't get that kind of commentary on network television. Jerry makes it easy to understand what's happening on the court, and you get the sense that he's having a great time doing his job. And you'll have a great time reading about his 20 years with the Kings.

CHAPTER ONE

The Pump-Station Hoodlums

If you saw the movie *Hoosiers*, you have an idea where I come from and why basketball is such a big part of my life. Although the movie took many liberties with the truth—to be honest, a lot of it was just plain made up—it painted a picture of just how important high school basketball is in small-town Indiana. While I've lived in Sacramento the last two decades, I'm proud to be a Hoosier—the second most famous native of French Lick, Indiana. I hope that if I'm not as well known as Larry Bird, maybe I'm better looking.

Hoosiers followed the miraculous story of a team from Hickory, Indiana. One minor detail: There is no Hickory, Indiana. But there are many places just like it. *Hoosiers* is really the story of Milan High School, which is about 60 miles east of French Lick. In Indiana, all the schools, regardless of their size, play in a tournament at the end of the season to determine the state champion. The tournament has been known to cause mass hysteria, especially when there are big upsets. That was the case the year Milan beat Muncie Central 32-30 for the championship.

1

It was 1954, and I was in fourth grade. Milan had about 120 students. Muncie Central was huge, something like 3,000 students. It was the first game that I ever saw on TV. In fact, we had just bought our first television set. I remember my father saying, "Come here and watch this, something's going on here." Bobby Plump was the star for Milan. Muncie Central's star was a junior named Gene Flowers. He would later be my high school coach.

The interesting thing is, the Milan coach, Marvin Wood, had been fired by French Lick High School three years before coaching Milan to the championship. Many of the old guys around French Lick would say, "Well, he couldn't coach against a zone." They didn't want to admit that they'd screwed up and fired the guy who coached one of the greatest upsets of all time.

When I was growing up—and it's still true to some degree today in the smaller towns—basketball almost was a religion. I saw my first high school basketball game when I was in second grade. My dad took me to see my uncle play—his name was Richard Morgan. The little gym was packed, and French Lick was playing West Baden. The two schools were a couple of miles from each other, and they were archrivals. I was just infatuated. I remember seeing them run onto the court in their uniforms and white shoes and thinking, "Wow, if I could ever play basketball for the high school … that would be the ultimate."

Although this will seem like a rural exaggeration, it's true: Going to French Lick for a basketball game was a big deal. I was country. When I was very young, we were in a little house about a quarter mile outside of Hillham, a town of maybe 100. Hillham itself was about five miles west of French Lick, and French Lick was a big city as far as I knew. That's where you went on Saturday to see all the humans and marvel at the two-story buildings and things like that.

French Lick was a resort town back then, maybe about 2,000 people. It's in an area called Spring Valley, and there are natural springs all around. They used to bottle "Pluto Water" there. The water was a natural laxative, and the company's motto was, "When nature won't, Pluto will." It smelled like sewage to me—sulfur water.

But people used it, and from what I hear, it cleaned you out pretty good.

Pluto, you may know, was the Greek god of the underworld, and the bottles of water had little red devils on them. French Lick High School's nickname was the Red Devils. West Baden, the other little local high school, was the Sprudels. I don't know if it's German or Dutch, but a Sprudel is a demon. It was a strange nickname, but then most high schools in that area don't have what you'd call traditional mascots. There were the Ireland Spuds. Don Buse and Gene Tormohlen played for the Holland Dutchmen. Marengo High School was the Cavemen, because there were bunches of caves around there. Vincennes High was the Alices because there was a story written in the '20s called Alice of Old Vincennes. There were the Washington Hatchets, the Bedford Stonecutters, the Frankfort Hot Dogs, and the Winslow Eskimos. John Wooden played for the Martinsville Artesians. I guess there are many artesian wells in that area. One of my favorites was the Fort Branch Twigs. I can just hear the cheerleaders shouting, "Go, Twigs!" or the opposing team saying, "Let's go snap those twigs!"

French Lick is tiny by most standards, but it was big time compared to some of those towns. There were two big hotels and two golf courses in the area for people who came for the water. The Springs Hotel in French Lick had about 800 rooms. The hotel in West Baden had about 400 rooms. It claimed to be one of the world's largest unsupported domes. The dome still exists. It was a Jesuit college for a while. Back in the 1920s, there was a ton of legal gambling in the area. Supposedly, Al Capone and other Chicago gangsters were involved.

We lived outside of Hillham until I was about seven. If Al Capone had ever knocked on our door looking to use the bathroom, he would have had to go out back and use the outhouse. We had a two-bedroom house about the size of one of Greg Ostertag's shoes. It didn't have running water, so there was no indoor plumbing. We had electricity, but it wasn't in every room. The bedroom that my brother, two sisters, and I shared wasn't wired. I had two older sisters, Mary Ann and Sharon, and two younger brothers, Jeff and

Randy. Randy was in Larry Bird's high school class. I was a senior in high school when Randy was a first-grader.

My dad was Ezra Ale Reynolds. He went by Ale. My mother was Bennice Owens. She was the youngest of 14 kids. She had a twin sister, Bernice—Bennice and Bernice. Bernice didn't look a thing like my mother, who was the youngest twin by an hour. My father was somewhere in the middle of a brood of eight kids. I don't remember everyone on his side of the family. They went their own ways. But Mom's family had reunions every year in Cuzco, Indiana—maybe 10 miles from French Lick.

I was born in 1944, and when I was very young, my father was shoveling coal in Jasper, about 15 miles away. Our house was on six acres, and we had a garden and all kinds of animals—a cow, pigs, chickens, and the whole deal. One of my jobs was to go out every morning and gather the eggs. Mom pretty much made everything. She made clothes out of old feed sacks.

Even as a little boy, I figured out that the way we were living was tough. I knew I didn't want to live that way my whole life. For about a year, my father was out of a job. He just did whatever odd jobs he could find. It was a tough existence, and we didn't have much. When people talk about poverty, I understand that a little bit. We definitely lived it. I used to go out and recruit poor inner-city kids when I was coaching in small colleges, and I never went into a house any poorer than the one in which I was raised. Now, we had a good family; we just didn't have much besides each other.

The first school I went to had four grades in one room and four in another. It didn't have electricity or indoor plumbing. But when I was in second grade, my dad got a job with Texas Eastern natural gas pump station, and he worked there until he retired. He made a decent living, and we had a company house. There were eight houses—they all looked the same—and the employees rented them. We had a yard, a garage, two bedrooms, gas, heat, electricity, and all that. We were living better than most people were.

Growing up, I can't say I ever felt destitute or poor. Most people were in the same boat. I never knew we were poor until we got our first TV set. The thing about television is, you start seeing what it's like for people who have money, people who have different lives than you. By that time, our family was doing much better. We were in the country, in a little house, but it was home.

We were three or four miles out of French Lick, and one of the high school coaches gave us the nickname "Pump-Station Hoodlums." We really weren't hoodlums, certainly not like some kids are today. He meant it affectionately, and the nickname became a badge of honor. I was the oldest boy in our little eight-house neighborhood, and there were eight boys in that compound. All of them were athletes, and I still contend that I was the best. Of course, I've always been especially modest. I really believe from the 1960s to the late '70s, one of us hoodlums was a key member of the Springs Valley High School Blackhawks, and the team was always good. I was one of the first kids from outside of town to play on the team. Before me, the team's best players were always from town. From that point on, most of the stars were from outside of town, and there was some resentment about that.

By the time I was in high school, French Lick and West Baden—the Red Devils and Sprudels—had consolidated to form the Springs Valley High School Blackhawks. The merger pulled the communities together through the past bitterness. They hated each other. I'm not exaggerating—that was the real deal. The consolidation caused some major controversies at first: Who was going to coach the team? What would the team colors be? People were asking questions like, "Why would they have three West Baden boys starting and only two French Lick boys starting?"

Of course, the answer was that the coach was starting the best players, which is a valid reason. Once they started winning, it all worked out and everyone relaxed. The first year, 1958, the Blackhawks went to the state final four. It was a miracle year, almost like *Hoosiers*. They were 25-0 when they lost to Fort Wayne South, which had a seven-footer named Mike McCoy. Fort Wayne South would later graduate a young lady named Dodie Kessler, who became my wife.

I graduated in 1962. I was probably the most underachieving person in my family, but I was a good student, probably top 10 in my class. There were about 350 students in four grades at Spring Valley and 88 in the graduating class. The school is actually smaller now than when I was there. The area's population is still the same, but there are fewer young people with families. There's nothing for kids there. I had the worst study habits—if it didn't come easy, I didn't bother with it much. I had good grades without working too hard.

I was a good all-around athlete. I think I still own the school record for most varsity letters, 11. I played basketball, baseball, and track. The furthest our basketball team ever reached was the sectionals, though, which was a disappointment. My senior year, they built a new gym for the high school that had 3,000 seats and is in use to this day. Some of the small schools in Southern Indiana had gyms that sat 7,000, and the high school gyms up north are bigger.

In the spring sometimes I'd have a track meet and a baseball game the same day. I usually played shortstop. In track, I broad-jumped 19-something and ran the half-mile in 2:07, not bad at that time. I also ran the 440 sometimes. We didn't have football; they started that as a JV program my senior year. There were no female sports at all then. I got a blanket as an award to commemorate my athletic achievements when I graduated. I was the best athlete in school history. Of course, Springs Valley didn't have much history then.

One of the best things about making the varsity basketball team when I was a sophomore was the road trips—we'd eat team meals at The Villager, which was the main restaurant in town. There were restaurants in the hotels, of course, but the locals never ate there. No one had that kind of money. Going to The Villager was a big deal for me. Until that first team meal, I'd never eaten in a restaurant.

I remember being very nervous the first time I went there. My mom thought I was nervous about the game, being young and playing against the varsity for the first time. But that wasn't the reason— I knew I could play and hold my own, but dinner concerned me. I didn't know how to order at a restaurant. As it turned out, it wasn't a problem because we didn't order. They just brought the food. I guess it's like learning to use an indoor toilet—I learned that quickly, though, and it's still one of the greatest things ever. In second grade, I started going to school in town. They had indoor toilets at school, so I'd hold it all morning long so I could go at school. Holding it was a challenge sometimes, because that bus ride could get bumpy.

I didn't have any hobbies aside from athletics, really. I was in student government: class president for three years. I always felt like I had some natural leadership abilities—even if they weren't always put to the best use. At the pump station, I was always the guy who organized the baseball and basketball games. We'd play at school, and then we'd have our own league. We kept stats and played in a barn loft. The rim was a little low, but I think that's how we all learned to shoot. We all had good technique. If you put too much arc on the ball, it hit a beam. All of us looked forward to playing in the games at the barn. We wanted the coaches at school to hurry up and get practice over so we could play in the *real* games.

When I was in high school, the big thing to do was to go drive "the circle" through French Lick and West Baden. It was like *American Graffiti* on a much smaller scale. There was a movie theater in town—the Dream Theater—that had films on weekends. Aside from that there wasn't much to do but drink beer and flirt with girls, although I didn't do too much of either as a teenager. I just liked to play ball. One decent outdoor court had lights on the main drag of town. The guys who were athletes would be there year-round, and there were always crowds watching.

Most of the people I went to school with realized that to accomplish very much in life, you'd have to leave French Lick. There weren't many great opportunities there. You could live decently on a little money. The high school principal might have been the second or third wealthiest person in town. That's one of the reasons I was interested in education.

However, French Lick was such a comfort zone that many of my peers didn't want to leave. They'd go away maybe to try to work or go to school and quit because it was too easy to come back. I almost did it. I could just hang out with my buddies, go to high school ballgames—that definitely happened to most guys. "Everybody knows me, I'm sort of a big deal," they think. Of course, that soon goes away, as they find out later. They try to relive it, but nobody cares.

Some of my classmates did okay for themselves. For example, A.R. Carnes, who played on the varsity with me and went on to play in college, is an executive with Getty Oil and is almost ready to retire.

When people ask me how a little hick town like French Lick produced two NBA lifers like Larry Bird and me, I always tell them:

"Must be something in the water."

Larry Bird, my son Jay, and me at home in Roseville.
Courtesy of Jerry Reynolds

CHAPTER TWO

"I Want To Hold Your Hand"

Before anyone ever heard of Larry Bird, I knew the Bird family. Larry was much younger than I was, so the only thing I knew about him at the time was that he was a little-bitty shit who always hung around. He had two older brothers—Mark and Mike—who I knew. They are also younger than I am. Mark was a good player; he played college ball. He'd hang around the court on the main drag. The Birds were poor. I think their circumstances were very similar to my family is. I can't say I'd walked a mile in Larry's shoes, but I knew that road very well.

When I was a hot shot in high school, Larry was in first or second grade. He didn't know who I was from a load of coal. The first time I talked to him was when the Kings played the Celtics. He told me he remembered my brother Jeff. Jeff's team at Spring Valley wasn't any good, but they got lucky and caught lightning in a bottle in the state tournament and went to the Sweet 16. By the time Larry got to high school, I'd heard through my brother Randy that Larry had developed into a good player, and I followed his career closely. I didn't know he was going to be one of the all-time greats or anything. But by then, he knew me because of Randy and because I was a college coach, which had some significance in French Lick.

9

I never wanted to be a coach. You might say I became one by accident.

My goal was to be a teacher. When I got out of high school, my hero was a guy named Phil Summers, who was a history teacher at Springs Valley High School. He came there my junior year. He seemed to have a great life. He was living in town, had a nice little house on a street, and drove a late-model used car. He came to work in a coat and tie. I thought that was cool. Teachers were highly respected at that time, and I couldn't imagine a better life than that.

I was the first person in my family to go to college. My parents didn't understand why I wanted to go. They thought that maybe I should go for a couple of years and then try to get a job. Once they realized that I was serious about wanting to be a teacher, they were very supportive. They didn't have very much money, but they gave me a little, and I earned scholarships, borrowed some money, and somehow got through it.

Once I graduated from high school, I went to Vincennes University Junior College. That's actually the name of it. I realize it sounds strange. Originally, it was *the* Indiana University. Vincennes was the capital of the Northwest Territories before Indiana became a state and was the capital of Indiana for a stint before Indianapolis. But the first college was there, before the state university was located in Bloomington. Vincennes University then became a junior college but kept "university" as part of its name. I think that makes the students smarter—and I'm a good example.

I wanted to go to Evansville or Indiana University, but they didn't want me at that time, probably with good reason. In my heart, if not in my head, I still felt I might become a big-time ballplayer. Branch McCracken, the coach at Indiana, had come down to French Lick to see me play, which was a big deal. Most people think that Bobby Knight was at IU forever. They forget that Branch won two NCAA championships with the Hoosiers before Bobby got there. Of course, the Indiana fans turned on Branch, too, when the team had a couple of down years.

Anyhow, Branch told me, "Well, if you go to a junior college and improve, we'll keep an eye on you, blah, blah, blah." I don't think they had any intention of doing that. IU probably told a hundred kids the same thing every year. It's like, "Go away, kid, you bother me. If you score a hundred points a game, yeah, we'll come back."

Well, I didn't score a hundred points per game. Honestly, I was just so-so. I started about half the time. They didn't have point guards then, just two guys playing guard, but I handled the ball mostly. Being asked to be the playmaker was a huge adjustment for me, since I was used to scoring. I could do it, but I really didn't want to. That was the big problem. I started more games as a freshman than I did as a sophomore, and part of the reason, in hindsight, was that I was too selfish at times. We had a couple of excellent inside players, and the coach wanted to go inside. I didn't understand why I should pound the ball inside when I was open and had a perfectly good shot from 25 feet. My motto always was: "If it feels like leather, shoot it."

We had a good coach and good teams despite the fact that my talents weren't featured as prominently as they should have been—or maybe because of that fact. I had a good experience there. We were something like 22-6 the first season I was there, and the second year we lost only three or four games and ended up ranked second nationally. We were upset in the regional round of the national tournament.

Partway through my second year—with probably 10 or 12 games to go in the regular season—was when that accident I mentioned earlier happened. In some ways, it was the worst thing that ever happened to me. In some ways, it was the best.

I don't like to talk about it very much, even 40 years later. It was late in the Christmas break. I'd been playing ball, and a couple of guys I knew—David Watts, the driver, and David Sugarman—offered me a ride home. They'd been drinking a little. Jargo Jones, a good friend of mine, and I were in the back seat. I knew right away that getting in that car was a mistake. I told them, "You have to stop this car and let me out," as if I knew something bad was going to happen.

You know how it is with teenagers and young adults: They think they're immortal. I know I probably did stupid things like that once or twice myself. We were out in the country on a gravel road. The conditions weren't that bad or anything, but they were just taking chances, being reckless. Maybe they were showing off for me a little. We were in a '55 Chevy. It was 1964, and "I Want To Hold Your Hand" was playing on the radio—just one of those stupid things you remember. We just rolled over again and again. Of course, no one wore seat belts in those days. I remember thinking, "Is this thing ever going to quit flipping?"

When we finally did stop flipping, I thought, "Well, I'm probably gone." I was bleeding badly. My back was hurt. I had some cracked vertebrae, although I didn't know that at the time, of course. My ear was almost cut off, and I had many gashes in my head from the glass in the side window. Some people came by, and I heard them say, "One's dead, and it looks like these two other ones are goners." One of the "other ones" they were talking about was me. I was going to die! They were just people, but I thought they might know something. They just saw all the blood, but I was convinced. I remember going in the ambulance to the hospital and thinking, "Is this how you feel before you die?"

As it turned out, David Watts died instantly. David Sugarman was partially paralyzed. He ended up killing himself later. Jargo was banged up, but not as bad as I was. I was 19 at the time. I spent a couple of weeks in the hospital, and then I had to wear a back brace for several months, so I couldn't participate in anything physical until June or July. They didn't really know what to do about things like that back then. They were concerned about cracks in the vertebrae, spinal cord damage, and all that. So they gave me some exercises to do, told me to stay away from trampolines and bull riding, and said that if everything went okay, I'd be almost as good as new in six months. It all worked out. I haven't had a back problem since. I don't have back pain or anything. That's amazing to me. I always assumed that I'd have a ton of back problems. I do have a ton of problems, but not back problems.

That accident had a big impact on my life, to be sure. It made me take some different steps. I didn't know it at the time, but I'd never play competitive basketball again. In a sense, though, that worked out fine, because I received an opportunity to coach.

Before the accident, I had accepted the fact I wasn't going to continue my playing career at Indiana or Evansville. But there were some schools, like Ball State and Eastern Illinois, that wanted to recruit me. The accident ended any notion I had that I'd go to even a mid-major program. I was looking at Findlay College in Findlay, Ohio—where Pittsburgh Steelers quarterback Ben Roethlisberger is from—because A.R. Carnes, my pal from high school who became an oilman, was up there.

My brother Jeff played well in high school, and he was going to Oakland City College, a small Baptist school between Vincennes and Evansville. Their coach, a guy named Delbert Distler, told me that if I'd come with Jeff, we'd have the chance to play together once I regained my health. Jeff and I had become rivals when he was in high school. Even though playing with him wasn't as big a deal as the coach might have thought, Oakland City College was starting to look pretty good, so I signed on. Jeff lived in the dorm, while I lived with some other guys in a little house off-campus.

My career at Oakland City College didn't get much farther off the ground than Vlade Divac could. Before the season started, Distler quit and became the superintendent of one of the area high schools. Willis Simpson was the new coach. He was a good guy and a good coach, but he wanted to bring in his own players, and I really couldn't blame him. My brother transferred to East Texas. Of course, I wasn't ready to play yet. I wasn't ready until that season was all but finished.

It was 1965, and I was 21 years old. Coach Simpson was willing to honor my scholarship, but he wanted me to commit to play two years. I had extra eligibility due to the accident, even though I was a senior academically. Honestly, I was a better player than anybody else there. I played intramurals and pick-up games against the varsity and the freshmen. None of them could guard me with a club, and everyone there knew it. I even scored a few against Jerry Sloan in the Tri-State Independent Tournament when he was at Evansville.

Still, I didn't see any reason to keep playing at Oakland City College. If I could graduate on time, I didn't want to stay around an extra year just to get my eligibility. I didn't have any academic problems, so it didn't make any sense. I wanted to get a good job and move on. Besides, it wasn't as if we were playing on national television. I would have been playing in front of 500 people. Really, small college basketball in Indiana ... most people are more interested in watching the local high school. I might have been decent there, but I didn't have any real desire. I could live without being a regional third-team all-doofus player.

Fortunately, Coach Simpson gave me another option. He told me that I could remain on scholarship without playing if I'd coach the freshman team. I was just a kid in college, a couple of years older than the freshman players were; but he needed someone to do it, and I needed to finish college and get on with my life. I had taken coaching classes, so Coach Simpson felt I had more going for me than most of the guys. "If you do this," he said, "it might help you out down the line." This turned out to be true. Some people might have thought that was a bad deal, but I didn't have any problem with it. I figured maybe I'd be a high school coach, and this would be good experience. I think I looked at it the right way.

I had never coached before on any level, so I did what most people do when they don't have any experience: I went back to my personal experiences as a player in junior college. I played for coach Allen Bradfield at Vincennes. When I was there, I hated the offense—but it made more sense when I was actually coaching, so I used much of it. We ran a lot of the old Cincinnati Bearcats stuff when Ed Jucker was coaching there—the swing and go and the backdoor trap series. We had 12 games and went something like 9-3. We won a couple of games against other four-year schools' freshman teams and played some junior colleges: not Vincennes, because they were too good, but some business schools. I should have scheduled some cosmetology schools and beefed up our record.

I found out quickly that I enjoyed coaching. The guys played pretty hard. One thing I did learn is that even if you did things wrong, you probably had a good chance for success if you really tried hard. I remember drawing up a play in one game when we were down a point late. We totally screwed up the play, but the guys really were working to run something, and we ended up getting a shot and winning the game. I was like, "I'll be damned. There *is* something to all the fuss I've been hearing about effort." We eventually got to the point where, even though I wasn't very much older, the guys more or less respected me. Of course, most of them knew I was a much better player than they were, so that helped a little. They were all little high school stars of that area. Most of them moved up from my team and played on the varsity. There were no All-Americans or anything, but they gave effort.

With that one season of experience under my belt, I was offered two jobs. I had a chance to take a high school job in Otwell, Indiana. I did my student teaching there, and they offered me a coaching job. I would have been the assistant there for the first year, then their head coach was going to retire, and I would take over. Otwell offered me $5,600. The other offer was to be an assistant coach under Allen Bradfield at Vincennes. I would also teach PE, but I had to start working on my master's degree right away. They offered me $5,500. I took less money, which is the smartest move I ever made.

Otwell is southwestern Indiana, between Vincennes and Evansville, a town at the time of maybe 500 people with no more than 200 students in the high school. It wasn't hard to turn that job down. I enjoyed my student teaching there, but even then I was smart enough to figure out that job wasn't likely to take me anywhere. Being head coach of the Otwell Millers ... I did not foresee greatness for myself. I assumed it would be—as it was for many of my friends in coaching—that I'd coach there for a few years and get fired. Then I'd go to Ireland and get fired. Then I'd go to Sheboygen a couple of years, and maybe if I got lucky, go up to the big time and get to Princeton: Princeton, as in Indiana, a town of 7,000—not the Ivy League school where Pete Carrill coached.

At last, I was big time!

CHAPTER THREE

A Wedding Ring and a Championship Ring

I was 21 or 22 when I started coaching at Vincennes, and I was there for five years. We were nationally ranked every year and were ranked #1 for at least some part of my last four seasons there, winning the national junior college championship in 1970 and 1972. I had a little something to do with that, because I was a good recruiter. Coach Bradfield recognized that I knew all the players—even when I was playing, I always read all the scouting reports and magazines. He recruited locally, and he was a good coach, so he could win—but he couldn't win nationally. So I would get all the recruiting guides. I called all the major schools to find out who they were after, whether they needed help on certain guys. Guys who went on to big-time pro careers like Bob McAdoo, Foots Walker, and Rickey Green became Vincennes Trailblazers.

Billy Packer was an assistant coach at Wake Forest at that time, and he gave me some help getting McAdoo. Wake wanted him, but the Atlantic Coast Conference had stricter entry requirements than the rest of the NCAA at the time. Mac could have gotten into the SEC or Big 10 or most of those places, so Wake was looking for a place to stash him and get his grades up.

Actually, we signed George McGinnis, Indiana's Mr. Basketball, and Roy Simpson, Kentucky's Mr. Basketball, that same year. McAdoo was considered maybe the third best player of the three. McGinnis never played for us. He paid his own way to go to Indiana University and waited until he became eligible, if you can believe that. He played one year there and then went pro with the ABA. McAdoo was really better than he was. Simpson went to Furman after Vincennes and played for the Bulls for a stint. Can you imagine how good that team would have been with a front line of McAdoo, McGinnis, and Simpson?

I learned a lot from Coach Bradfield. He was a brilliant man who was flawed. He could be difficult and had a drinking problem, but he had brains. He was a mathematician out there coaching against P.E. majors. We got along pretty well, for most of my five years there.

When I was coaching at Vincennes I made friends with a high school coach from Lawrenceville, Illinois, named Ron Felling. We played in pickup games, and once, after I blew by him, he said, "Man, you're like the Caucasian Comet." The nickname stuck with me over the years, although these days, I'm more like the "Caucasian Snail."

Another thing that has stuck with me is my wife, Dodie. I was teaching and coaching at Vincennes, and she was a student. I saw her and said, "Wooooo, I like that." I had a 1965 GTO convertible. When I signed a contract, that car was the first thing I bought. It was a year old with a purple-white interior—a great-looking car. I was a cool dude in French Lick and Vincennes both, but Dodie didn't seem very impressed by that. I stayed with it, though, and we finally started dating. It was probably my best recruiting job ever.

Now, a teacher dating a student would have been frowned upon back then, as it today, but we were very discreet. And she was only a year younger than me, so I wasn't exactly cradle-robbing. After high school, she had worked for a few years before going to college. We'd sneak around. We've been married 36 years, so I hope it's okay now.

We were hitched around Christmas time a year after we met in Fort Wayne. The day after the wedding, we went on our honeymoon: I had to scout a high school holiday tournament in South Bend. So Dodie was indoctrinated early, bless her heart. At first, we lived in a little apartment that used to be a garage, not a whole lot bigger than my current office. When our son Jay was born, we moved to a little house five or six miles outside of Vincennes on a watermelon farm. We had an oil-burning pot-bellied stove for heat. It would keep the kitchen and the little living room warm, but the farther away you got, in the bedroom or the bathroom, you didn't get much heat. Sometimes when it got cold, we'd have to break the layer of ice on top of the water in the toilet. We finally rented a house for $80 a month inside town and thought we were in hog heaven. We were warm, close to the university, and had plenty of room.

The Vietnam War was going on at this time, and I was very lucky to avoid the draft. Earlier, I had gotten a deferment because I was a teacher even though I was single. No, I didn't become a teacher to avoid Vietnam; I had made that decision long before. Then I was deferred for being married and having a baby on the way. Then they started drafting married guys and instituted the draft lottery—but it turned out that my birthday was lucky. Of course, I didn't have nearly as much luck with the lottery once I was with the Kings.

Those early years with Dodie probably went better than they should have, mainly because of her. She made it work. She stayed home and raised Jay. I was recruiting too much and drinking too much at times, but I wasn't running around on her or anything. She was great. I'd bring home uniforms and stuff to wash. I'd do things like clean the gym floor or paint the locker rooms, and she'd help with the equipment. That was life. That's what had to be done. I always taught, too, mainly P.E. I finished my master's at Indiana State in 1970, working evenings and during the summer.

I did a few hours of work toward my doctorate at IU, but in 1972 I got a chance to coach at West Georgia, a college with maybe 6,000 students near Atlanta that had a beautiful atmosphere. It's now a university. It was my first real split from French Lickdom. A few of the guys I had recruited to Vincennes—Foots Walker, Tommy Turner, and David Edmunds, all veterans of a national championship junior college team—came down there with me. West Georgia was a four-year school playing in the NAIA that had never been very good, maybe 14-13 the year before I got there. I brought in a few other junior college kids—Jerry Faulkner, Randy Roundtree, and Pat Magley—and we went to the national NAIA tournament the first year.

In 1974, we won the national small-college championship. I still wear the ring we got from the school. It was Foots Walker's senior year. We played Western Kentucky, a Division-I school that was solid, and beat them by 18-19 points in Bowling Green. At that time, we were definitely better than Georgia Tech or Georgia. We had better players. Four guys on that team were drafted.

Foots played about a decade in the NBA and had a nice career with Cleveland and New Jersey. None of the other guys made it in the NBA. Foots was special. We got him at West Georgia mainly because most people didn't realize how good he was. They were concentrating on recruiting bigger guys. It's the same old thing: coaches look at big klutzes who can't play and ignore the six-foot-one guys who really can.

Foots went to Southampton High School on Long Island, and I recruited him there. His team lost something like one or two games in three years. Then he went to junior college and maybe lost three games in two years and won a national championship. Then he came to West Georgia, and we maybe lost five or six games in two years and won a national championship. It was like, "Duh, you think he's a winner? Is there a correlation here?" He was just one of those guys who overachieved and was simply a winner.

After Foots graduated, I stayed one more year at West Georgia. We moved up to Division II, and we were beaten by the University of New Orleans in the regional tournament. Wayne Cooper, who is now the Kings' vice president of basketball operations, was a sophomore there at the time. They also had a guy named Wilbur Holland on that team who went on to play for the Bulls. It was probably the worst team we had at West Georgia, but it wasn't bad. It was a great game. We played in New Orleans and lost in overtime. I always kid Coop that they cheated us, which they did.

My next stop was Rockhurst College in Kansas City. Cotton Fitzsimmons and Phil Johnson helped me get that job. Cotton knew the athletic director really well, so I had an "in." I knew Cotton, who was coach of the Atlanta Hawks then, from Moberly Junior College in Missouri. His last year at Moberly was my first year at Vincennes. They had just finished winning two straight national championships, and he had gone to Kansas State as an assistant, then as head coach, then on to the Phoenix Suns and the Hawks. I knew Phil when I was at Vincennes. He was the head coach at Webber State, and I helped him with some recruits.

For the longest time, I hadn't really followed the NBA. It was on TV once a week, and to me, Indiana University was still the pinnacle of basketball. But I had come around, and they knew I wanted to get involved in the professional game at some point. Rockhurst wasn't a great job—it was a Jesuit school of about 3,000 that most people in town didn't seem to know existed—but I really wanted to get it. All the NBA teams practiced there, and the Kings held their camp there. I knew I'd have the opportunity to see all the NBA teams practice and help Phil in camps. I ended up staying at Rockhurst nine years. They hadn't had a winning team for seven or eight years. We had a winning record my first year. We never won a championship there, but we were nationally ranked six straight years in the NAIA.

I really enjoyed Rockhurst. It was located in the middle of the city, and it was the first time I really lived in an urban area. Dodie had earned her master's degree at the University of Missouri-Kansas City and taught special education. We didn't have the atmosphere at Rockhurst that we had at West Georgia. The gym only sat 1,500 or so, and we'd draw maybe 900 a game. We had to get legitimate student-athletes at Rockhurst. At Vincennes or West Georgia, my job was to get good basketball players and then try to help them any way possible with academics. At Rockhurst, our recruits had to be in the top third of their class, and it was very difficult to get transfers from junior colleges.

Still, I thought we had a good chance to win a national championship one year there—we went to the finals twice—but we had an injury to a key guy. When you have only five or six players who are good enough to win and then lose one of them, it's tough. We had four straight years with records like 24-6 or 24-5. We changed the team's image, and some of the better local players started looking at Rockhurst as a legitimate option. I recruited some kids who chose to go to Missouri, Kansas, or Creighton instead, but then they came back to Rockhurst if things didn't work out. I never kidded myself about being the best coach in the world, although I think I was pretty good. But if you want to win at the small-college level, the best thing to do is get some major college talent. There, the secret's out. One thing I'm very proud of is that everybody I coached graduated—100 percent in nine years. Maybe I didn't have the same level of player that I had at Vincennes or West Georgia, but I had good kids.

Then there was Danny King, one of the most memorable guys I ever recruited. He was a French Lick kid, and I got him to come down to West Georgia. After I left, he didn't want to stay there, and he ended up at Indiana State. Danny is one of the reasons that Larry Bird ended up there. "Dangerous Danny" was a good player, and several big schools recruited him. I tried to get him to go to Rockhurst with me, but I understood when he went back to Indiana.

Danny was two years older than Larry. He was kind of a leader early on for Larry. Fortunately, Larry didn't continue following him because Danny was definitely a big-time runner. He called himself "Catfish" King. He was tough. I remember one time when I was with him, we walked into some place—he might have been 28 or 29 and was a construction worker—and he says, "I'm Danny 'Catfish' King, six feet, 225 pounds of rompin', stompin' hell, and I can whip any man in here." Everyone just looked down into their beer—they didn't want any piece of him. I said, "Ooooo-kay." He had a little reputation, and it definitely was earned.

I became good friends with Phil Johnson when I was at Rockhurst. When he was fired, he came to some of our games, and he always told me that if he ever got another head coaching job in the NBA, he'd like to have me as an assistant. In the meantime, it came out that the Kings were leaving Kansas City. I was a little frustrated with that. They had stopped practicing at Rockhurst, and my NBA connection was gone. "So much for that," I figured. "Maybe I have to go find a little better college situation, a better chance to win a championship."

So I went to Pittsburg State, down in the southeast corner of Kansas. We were the Gorillas, and I'll never know how they came up with that nickname. The situation was similar to that in West Georgia. They had about 6,000 students, but they had a 6,000-seat arena. They hadn't had a winning team in 13 years. We had a winning season—16-14—and went to the playoffs. I had a decent recruiting year and could have been a little better next year.

Fortunately for me, though, Phil Johnson had come back late in the season to take over the Kings before they went to Sacramento. He called me in May or June and offered me a job as the second assistant. I said, "Yes, Sir."

CHAPTER FOUR

A Room of My Own

Now, I like money as much as the next guy, provided that the next guy isn't Donald Trump. But for the second time in my career I took less money to take a job I really wanted. Believe it or not, I earned less money to coach at the highest level of basketball in the world than I had earned at Pittsburg State.

The difference was only $3,000, but I didn't realize the extent of what that meant until I arrived in Sacramento. There's a big difference between the cost of living in California and living in Kansas. You can live pretty well on $40,000 a year in Pittsburg, Kansas: a 3,000-square-foot house on about an acre of land was going for maybe $75,000 at that time. In Sacramento, we found a house we could afford in a nice neighborhood near one of the best high schools in town. It was 1,300 square feet. It was smaller than we were used to, but it was nice. The best thing is, there was tons of traffic out in front of the house. We didn't have to worry about salesmen. We didn't have much of a yard, and they'd have been run over if they'd stood on our front porch.

Sacramento is my home, and I've enjoyed living here the last 20 years. But my first impressions weren't the most favorable. The first thing that struck me was how brown and hot it was. I was surprised by that. Sacramento in July, and it was hot. Imagine that. I was used to a lot of humidity, and at least they don't have to deal with that in Sacramento. The other thing that struck me right away was how many houses in Sacramento didn't have cable TV. It was probably the only major city in America that didn't have cable TV by then. I mean, they had cable TV in Pittsburg, Kansas, and even in Vincennes and French Lick. That should have been a pretty good clue about the political aspect of this particular city and how it takes forever to do logical, nominal things … building a new arena, for example. It reminded me of going back to the '50s. I'd be driving down the street and notice all the TV antennas.

Back then, I thought Sacramento was much like Omaha with a great climate. It didn't have much of a downtown, hardly any buildings over 10-12 stories tall. Since then, of course, there has been tremendous growth, and Sacramento looks a lot more like a major-league city, with more to come. Quite honestly, in 1985 it was very unimpressive for what's considered a major market.

When I first got here, the first Arco Arena wasn't even done. The skyline, such as it was, was off in the distance to the south. We had our offices in a little cookie-cutter kind of buildings across the street from the arena, and we'd go across occasionally and look at the progress. But there was nothing else out there for maybe three miles going toward I-5. Now there's Arco II and all kinds of buildings and homes. I remember Reggie Theus going pheasant hunting out there where human beings live now. It was legal. There was no danger to anyone, just wide-open spaces.

The first responsibility I had for the Kings was coaching a summer league team. As I mentioned, I came out to Sacramento in July. I always get a kick out of being blamed for drafting Joe Kleine. I've gotten that every year for the last 20 years. The draft was held a couple of weeks before I signed a contract, so I tell people, "You can blame me if you want, but I had nothing to do with that."

That summer league seemed to last forever—one week in Seattle, one week in the Bay Area, one week in Portland, and one week in Sacramento. I lived at what was called the Woodlake Inn at the time (it's now the Radisson). During the regular season, we stayed in Red Lions and Marriotts—to me that was big time. They were nice hotels. We stay in much swankier places today. But I had my own room! In college, it was always at least two to a room for players and coaches. We'd stay at a Red Roof Inn and places like that, which seemed all right at the time. The per diem when I came into league was probably $50 or $60 a day. I was coming from a small college where I was used to living on the road for $12 a day and had to show receipts to get it. Unfortunately, I couldn't eat $50 worth of food a day, but I could drink it up. That was a concern. Fortunately, I don't drink at all now. Anyhow, it was all very impressive to me at first. It's like anything—you get used to it at some point.

The people in Sacramento treated me well from the get-go. Of course, I was the second assistant, so I was kind of a non-entity, and most people didn't even know who I was. One of the first big community deals they had to welcome the team—I can't remember if it was the state or local government or the chamber of commerce—they didn't have enough seats up on the stage. The late Bill Jones, the trainer at the time, and I didn't count. We had a little table in the back, like the kids' table at Thanksgiving. Obviously, I was a real big deal in Sacramento from day one.

Actually, I was thrilled to death to be in the NBA. We had a good staff—Phil Johnson, and the lead assistant, Frank Hamblen—and I learned a ton. Phil has been Jerry Sloan's right-hand man on the Utah Jazz bench since leaving the Kings in December 1988. He would have been a very successful head coach had he pursued any of the opportunities that came his way, but he seemed very content in Utah, and I'm happy for him. Frank is a career top assistant coach who became the head coach of the Lakers last year—pretty much a thankless, impossible job. Those guys really showed me the ropes. I was just overwhelmed to be in the NBA, like so many guys who come from college.

I'd been around some quality players in college, but when you come into the pro level, you're just amazed by the talent. It was certainly a jolt, even though I'd watched many NBA practices. Phil told me that it was going to take a while to realize that while all our guys were really, really good, they weren't necessarily good enough to help us win at the highest level. They were all great college players who helped their teams win. Despite Phil's warning, I fell in love with all of our players. Then we started playing preseason games, and it was like, "Whoa, Phil was right: The other teams' guys are better than our guys. How'd that happen?"

I think that's why many college coaches—even big-name guys who become head coaches—struggle. Almost invariably, they need to be assistant coaches for a few years. I understand why they don't: They can't afford to, because of both the pay and their reputations. In most cases, if they're serious about a long-term career in the NBA, they'd benefit from learning the league. You have to learn that certain things you swear by in college don't work as well in the pros— that the level of talent that wins for you in college doesn't win in the NBA. Grown, multimillionaire men must be dealt with differently than college students. Even a guy like Mike Montgomery—as good a coach and as smart as he is—could have used some time on an NBA bench before becoming the head guy.

As far as coaching goes, there's not much new under the sun. Everyone runs more or less the same stuff, college or pro, with some different wrinkles. The difference is that there's far more coaching done in the NBA—as far as game preparation and game adjustments—than there is at the college level. Now, I know all the Dick Vitales and the Billy Packers will go nuts over that statement, but they don't know what they're talking about. It's a different game. The NBA players are so skilled—they simply can do more things than college players. Therefore, as a coach, you have to do more.

The simplified version is this: Bobby Knight is a great college coach. Well, he had a way that he's going to defend the pick and roll from the first game of the season to the last. That's how the Hoosiers were going to do it, no matter whom they're playing. No disrespect to Bobby, but if you're going to guard the Lakers' pick and roll with Magic Johnson and James Worthy one way for a whole game, they'll never have to run another play. They'll beat you with that play, so you'd better have three or four different ways to defend it. You might

Giving brilliant, but futile instructions to Joe Kleine and Rodney McCray.
Tim DeFrisco/NBAE/Getty Images

have to use them all in one quarter just to avoid embarrassment. They'll still beat you with it, because they're that good.

In the NBA, there are more decisions—I'd guess three times as many as in college. Sometimes the skill level makes it seem like no one is coaching. For example, look at tapes of Pat Riley's teams with the Lakers. Riley was great with his early offense. I remember seeing it for the first time as a scout and being blown away. It was choreographed so well. Magic looked like he was freelancing, but he wasn't. He was looking for specific things, and it just happened so easily and so smoothly that 90 percent of the people watching thought it was simply schoolyard basketball. But it was the combination of a plan that everyone bought into and a high level of talent—a situation where they could actually do what the coach asked them to do, which isn't always the case. Some players can't do what the coach wants, and others won't. When great coaching and great players work together, though, you get great teams that are wonderful to watch, and they win championships.

As a coach, you have to find a way to adjust to the great talent, and that's part of the difference between college and the NBA. The way I've always looked at it, when Bobby Knight was at Indiana, it was Bobby Knight and the Indiana Hoosiers. When Phil Jackson coached at Chicago—it was Michael Jordan and the Chicago Bulls. It wasn't K.C. Jones and the Boston Celtics—it was Larry Bird and the Boston Celtics. You don't pay $60 to watch Jerry Sloan or Rudy Tomjanovich coach, regardless of how good they are. You're paying to watch great players do things that the average fan can't do in his wildest dreams. The great coaches in the NBA know that. The trick is to have one of those great players.

Unfortunately, we didn't have one when I first joined the Kings. Back then, I did much more scouting than actual coaching. My main responsibility was what these days they'd call a video coordinator. We didn't have a video department then; so I would take game tape and break it down to find specific plays to focus on. I did all the advance scouting. If we were going to play the Portland Trail Blazers, I'd go see them and learn their basic plays as well as I could. I'd get tapes of their games and try to match up what I'd seen with some of those tapes and present a taped five- or six-play segment in practice to get the defense ready. The Kings gave me two VCR and I did all the tapes at home. My son Jay would help me. I think the players paid attention, for the most part, because we didn't overdo it. Most teams do these days. There's such a thing as too much information. It's paralysis by analysis. But back then we didn't have much, and the players appreciated what we had.

I was with the team as much as possible and tried to help with player development. Oh, and I refereed, too, although the real referees discouraged that. I traveled an unbelievable amount, but I still was probably with the team 75 of the 82 games. If I knew then what I know now, I wouldn't have come into the NBA. I would have stayed at Pittsburg State. Don't get me wrong: I'm grateful I got the job, but it was a challenge. I just did my best to get through it, and it helped me a great deal.

Being a pro scout is probably the best way to learn the league. I scouted in college, but it's much more precise in the pros. I'd say it took me half a season to become what I consider a competent scout. Phil and Frank were very patient with me and helped me learn. Anybody can scout colleges, because that just comes down to offering an opinion, and there aren't nearly as many games. Advance pro scouting, well, there are many former jocks who may be leading franchises now who couldn't be advance scouts. You have to have the Xs and Os and the terminology, and you have to be able to think on your feet. When you're watching a play, you have to see it, react to it, draw it up, and remember it.

The worst part of scouting is the traveling. It's just grueling. I always tell my wife, I may not know many things, but I know how to pack. Beyond just waking up and trying to remember what city you're in, you have to learn your way around. The first time you go to, say, Seattle, where do you stay? Is it better to be at the airport or downtown? How do you get to the arena when you're on your own? What door do you go to at the arena to pick up your pass? Where's the pressroom where you get your pregame meal? You have to learn hundreds of little things that you wouldn't normally think of to make life on the road easier.

Once you've done it once or twice in each city, it's okay. But the first time, it's always a pain. I remember my first trip to the Boston Garden to scout. I caught a cab from the airport, which was surprisingly close, maybe a $6 fare. Those East Coast cities are crammed. The guy dropped me in front of some cruddy storefront, and I said, "I wanted to go to Boston Garden!"

He told me to walk into a certain door, then he took off, leaving me there with my finger up my nose. I went in the door—this was a couple of hours before tip-off, so there was no one around—and the walkway wound around and around, and all of the sudden I was at the pass gate. I expected to see this beautiful building (it's a garden, right?), and it was just a strange, skuzzy old building. But once I got inside the actual arena, there was that famous atmosphere: the parquet floor, the championship banners and all that. That season, the Celtics lost exactly one home game, and that was the one I saw. The Portland Trail Blazers beat them. I went in afterward to talk to Larry. Of course, he wasn't in a real good mood, so I didn't hang around too long.

I have to admit that I was a little scared the first time I went to New York City. I was a small-town guy scouting the league for the first time. Fortunately, I was with the team on that trip, because I would have been lost if I was on my own. Still, I hardly left my hotel room. I just assumed that I'd be mugged if I went outside. I'd be staring up at the skyscrapers and someone would bonk me on the head and take my wallet and all my clothes, for sure. Poor little Jerry from French Lick would be walking down Broadway trying to cover up his naked butt. The last few years, I've really enjoyed going to New York. But it took me four or five years before I left the confines of the hotel to maybe find a deli or someplace to eat. In New York, you can go through your per diem pretty fast if you stay in the hotel. There can't be too many places in the world where you pay $10 for toast and coffee.

Visiting Boston Garden and Madison Square Garden—those places stick out in my mind because most of the games tend to run together.

I say, "tend," because there were a couple of times in that first season that I'll never forget.

One was our win at home over Boston. That's when the Celtics were about at their peak. Larry missed two free throws down the stretch, and that helped us win. That was probably the first and last time I saw Larry Legend miss two in a row, and you had better believe I gave him some grief after the game.

Secondly, of course, was opening night. There were fans wearing tuxedos, a string quartet playing at the main entrance, and Commissioner Stern was there. The pizzazz of the whole thing was something. The building had been completed. I think they'd used it once before our first game, a Bobby Chacon fight a week before. They didn't have the seats all marked or anything. It was just absolute chaos. They were still painting and hammering. Of course, we blew the game down the stretch. We had a nice lead, but the Clippers beat us. Derek Smith had a huge game, which probably led to another problem later.

CHAPTER FIVE

Someone Should Put Up a Statue

Our first training camp was held at Yuba College in Yuba City, a bit north of Sacramento. Training camp was real— two-a-days, mile runs—the whole nine yards. Our players today probably would revolt at something like that. If the two-a-days didn't get them, the accommodations would have. We stayed at a Best Western Motel called the Bonanza Inn, which was fine to me, but it sure wasn't the Ritz. The only thing to do there was concentrate on basketball, which is the way it should be. At about that time, one of those phony baloney nationwide surveys rated Yuba City the worst place in the United States to live. At one practice, a guy came into the gym who looked like he was with the Hell's Angels. He said he had some friends outside who wanted to challenge the Kings to a game. Phil turned him down, and fortunately, they didn't ride into the gym on their hogs.

We only played four preseason games: one at American River College in Sacramento, one at University of Nevada at Reno, one at Yuba College, and one in Oklahoma City. The first couple of games were in gyms that maybe sat 1,500 or 1,800 people, and they were fanatical. We played the last game Oklahoma City against the Pacers because Wayman Tisdale, their top draft pick, was a big star at

Oklahoma. The only problem was, he hadn't signed. There might have been a couple of hundred people in the stands. In Sacramento, it seemed like we could draw a couple of hundred people to watch us run wind sprints. We had an intrasquad scrimmage at American River. It was about 110 degrees in the gym, and you couldn't even find a place to stand. I think the towel boys were signing autographs. That was one of the first indications that the Kings' relationship with Sacramento would be special.

The Kings were in Sacramento only because of a young developer named Gregg Lukenbill. He and his business partners bought the team when it was in Kansas City—really just by assuming the team's debts. The NBA wasn't exactly the multimillion-dollar enterprise it is these days, and guys with a relatively small fortune, like "Luke," could get involved. I didn't know anything much about owners, but I liked Luke. You could see he was an energetic, enthusiastic guy. He had a vision—sometimes I'm not sure a vision of what, and I think he might be the first to admit it. But he was remarkable in his drive.

Luke brought a professional sports team to a city that probably had no desire to have one. Before the Kings came to Sacramento, the biggest sporting events in town were Hangtown and the Pig Bowl— a motorcycle race and an annual charity football game between the police and sheriffs. Luke created the idea that Sacramento was a big-league city. He built two arenas even though the city fought him every step of the way. When he was building the first Arco—I think he was one of the first owners to get money from naming rights for the building—he told everyone it was a warehouse. He was trying to avoid the interference he expected on building an arena as long as possible.

His strengths far outweighed his weaknesses. Like the rest of us, Luke was flawed. He wanted to be part of the basketball decision-making process, but he'd probably admit now that he had no knowledge of basketball. Still, I've said this many times: If they build a statue of anybody in Sacramento, they ought to have one of Gregg Lukenbill in front of the arena or something. He won't be truly appreciated until enough years go by, then people will come to understand how he stuck his neck out and made things happen. There wouldn't be any Kings in Sacramento without him, and the city is a better place for having him as one of its citizens.

Luke hoped that the local government would let him develop the land around the arena, and that's how he'd get his investment back. All the land is houses, businesses, and whatnot now, but others, not Luke, reaped the benefits. Luke was ahead of his time, which unfortunately happens to most visionaries—whether it's politics, or business, or sports. The people who are out of the box, who see things differently, don't always benefit from it. That's Gregg Lukenbill. If he were an artist, he'd have cut off his ear by now.

That first Arco Arena, by the way, was something else. As I mentioned, it was barely ready for the first game. I'd been in high school gyms that were very similar in size. Maybe they sat 10,333 in bleachers rather than chair seats, but there weren't many other differences. The atmosphere was very similar to what I'd seen at Creighton or Indiana State or Bradley. The crowd was right on you, and, boy, were they loud. After that first-year win against the Celtics, Larry Bird admitted that the crowd had affected him, and he said it in a very complimentary way. The place was special, and we had a true home-court advantage. They duplicated it to some degree in the second arena, but you could never really get the same atmosphere. I don't think there's ever been anything like that in NBA history.

But everything was scaled-down. Even the home locker room wasn't much bigger than my office is now. I didn't think about it too much because I was from a small college, so I was used to that type of situation. However, I know the visitors' locker room was terrible. Many times, they'd dress at their hotel before coming to the arena. The visitors' training table was out in the hallway. The pressroom was a makeshift, cordoned-off area. Phil, Frank, and I shared a small office upstairs.

I didn't really know it at the time, to be honest, but looking back, to some degree we were doing things on a shoestring budget. We were probably well below the middle of the pack as far as scouting budgets and staffing. I was new to the NBA, so I didn't have anything to judge our situation against. Luke and his partners didn't have the deepest pockets in the league. Still, I know that Phil

Johnson—he was kind of an old-school coach—wasn't that concerned about it. His attitude was, "Tell me who the players are, and I'll coach them." As the years go on, that approach makes more sense. But we probably didn't have everything we should have had to have a better chance for success.

Luke owned the team, but Joe Axelson ran the basketball operations. He had been in the league office, had experience running several franchises, and probably assisted Gregg in taking control of the franchise in Kansas City. The transition couldn't have gone any smoother. Gregg realized Joe knew more about basketball than he did, even though most people criticized Joe over the years.

I really liked Joe. He was an old-school kind of guy who had come up through the NBA when the operation was much smaller—just a small collective business run by a few people. The league's evolution and transition ended up turning that strength into a weakness over time. The NBA started getting much bigger—the exposure, the salaries, everything. Scouting and coaching staffs were starting to change dramatically, and that may have been difficult for Joe. The world he knew had changed.

There weren't salary caps back when we started in Sacramento, and we spent no more than a couple of million dollars for all our players—not just for our third-string power forward. The league as a business started to explode about the time that the team came here, and that was tough for Joe and others who had been in the league for 20 years—just as it would be for people like myself 20 years from now. People view you as a dinosaur passed by an evolving world.

That first year, we may not have been a model franchise. But we did have a good group of players who played hard, were fun to watch, and clicked with the fans. That really got us off on the right foot in Sacramento. We didn't have any bad guys—no druggies, no one being arrested, no one taking fights up into the stands. Our guys weren't perfect, but collectively, they were as good as one could hope for in a new city and unfamiliar situation.

Before we had Mitch Richmond or Chris Webber, Reggie Theus was our big star. I really enjoyed the time I spend with Reggie. He was a great talent, still one of the most gifted players ever to play for this franchise. Now, Reggie certainly liked Reggie—he was extremely good and knew he was. Had he sacrificed a smidgeon of his individuality, he could have been much better. Although I enjoyed being around him, he could have done more to get along with his teammates. That being said, he honestly had Hall of Fame talent.

Sometimes players were jealous of Reggie because he was everything they all wanted to be: gifted, good-looking, intelligent, and personable. There were guys who resented him for having all those gifts. He could be headstrong. He knew all the plays, really studied them. Now, he'd still break those plays—he's the only guy I ever coached who would sometimes break his own plays. That was Reg. I always thought, looking back at the little stint I had with him as a head coach, that the best way to handle Reggie was to give him more responsibility. The more freedom he had in the system the better he was. For us, he was much more of a threat from the point than the shooting guard. I'm not saying he could lead you to a championship, but Reggie could do almost anything, and you had to let him. If you tried to put him in a box, he was going to find a way to get out.

One thing that people didn't understand about Reggie was that he was really a tough guy. Most people thought he was soft, because he was such a pretty boy. The guys in the league knew he was a tough buckaroo. They didn't mess with Reg. He came to play—he played hurt, and he practiced every day, unlike most stars. He didn't always practice well, but he was out there. Reg also worked on his game as the great ones do. I remember telling him as he was leaving the Kings that he'd need a three-point shot to hang on to his career in the league. He was really an 18- or 20-foot shooter, and he was losing some speed and quickness. So he worked on his three-point shot and got pretty good from that range. He was very much a professional.

If Eddie Johnson wasn't as big a star as Reggie was, he was one of the all-time great clutch shooters in this league—for us, certainly, but probably more so as his career ended up with Phoenix, Houston, and Seattle. He was a big-time shooter, and many people forget that he, not Reggie, was our leading scorer that first season. He always had the rap—I remember Joe Axelson saying this all the time—that he was a bad defender. Okay, he wasn't a real strong defender. But I

Reggie Theus drives to the hoop. *Bill Baptist/NBAE/Getty Images*

always thought, jeez, he's scoring 20, and the guy guarding him is scoring 18. If all the players did that, we'd probably win more often.

Eddie would get you 20 points in 30 minutes most nights and truly was the guy who wanted to take the big shot. He didn't make them all, but just like Mike Bibby these days, he didn't back down, and you knew the shot would be put up there with a chance. There wasn't an ounce of choke in Eddie. Aside from clutch shooting, Eddie proved after he left the Kings that he was the kind of guy who could fit into different systems, contribute to championship-caliber teams, and still be very valuable in lesser roles. He just found a way to contribute, and that's all you can ask of a player.

Larry Drew was our highest-paid player. He was a small guard, but he wasn't a true point guard. He could handle the ball, but Reggie was more of a playmaker. Larry actually had his best years before the Kings moved to Sacramento. There were a couple of seasons in Kansas City when Larry was an all-star-level guard. That's the reason he had the big contract at that time. He had some injuries and slowed down a little, although he was still a very solid player. I remembered him from Wyandot High School in Kansas City. He just astounded you back then. The game was easy for him. He was very smooth.

Mike Woodson, who was head coach of the Atlanta Hawks last year (Drew was one of his assistants), was "Mr. Fundamental." He was a Bobby Knight product, maybe the best I ever saw at using screens. He wasn't a great athlete, but he was consistently able to score because he kept moving and knew how to get open. He was a delight to coach and a great person. I'm not surprised at all that he became a head coach. He was one of those guys who always studied the films. He really knew his opponent. I think he was looking for an edge, because he knew he needed an edge. He outperformed guys who were more talented. Woody played hurt; he had bad wheels. He did everything he could that first year to help us get into the playoffs—and for his trouble, he got his butt traded, but that's a story for later.

Our big guys were LaSalle Thompson, Joe Kleine, Otis Thorpe, and Mark Olberding. They weren't exactly the Four Horsemen of the Apocalypse, but they all had different skills that added something to the team.

LaSalle was nicknamed "Tank," and not only for his toughness. Tank was one of the best defensive rebounders we've seen on the Kings—and maybe in the league. He was one of those guys who'd set great screens and rebound. He certainly wasn't the most gifted athlete, and he was a little undersized for a center, but Tank had a big heart. What he couldn't accomplish as a player was because he didn't have the skills, not because he didn't give the effort or didn't care. I always said that was what I admired about Tank: He maximized his potential. If he had a weakness, it was that he didn't study the game. He was a legitimately tough guy who was a good teammate. I think every one of his teammates would say, "Maybe he's not an all-star, but I sure like playing with him." He was unselfish to a fault.

Like Larry, Mark Olberding's career was winding down when we moved to Sacramento. He was Mr. Tough Guy. There were guys in the league who were scared of Dinger, and they should have been. He would turn out your lights. Between him and Tank, there were some screens set. I wish the current Kings could set picks like those guys, because they definitely could get some people open. I remember in more than one close game, Mark coming into the huddle and saying, "If you want Eddie open, I'll get him open," and I guarantee you he would have. It may not have been legal, but he'd get him open. We did have legitimate toughness. Joe Kleine was a disappointment to many people, but he was tough. We had shooters and guys who would set screens, and Mark was the leader of that pack. He was so good at it that a guy like Otis, who didn't like to set picks but was so gifted otherwise, got into that, too.

Joe Kleine and Otis were kind of interconnected. As I said, the fans—and honestly, the team—didn't think Joe ever lived up to our expectations. There was some pressure on him because he was the first ever draft pick in Sacramento. He had a big body and some skills, but he didn't have great hands. Actually, he had small hands for a big guy, and short arms. Joe was a seven-footer, but with his reach he was more like a six-foot-nine guy, as opposed to a Chris

LaSalle Thompson grabs a board. *Stephen Dunn/NBAE/Getty Images*

Webber, who's six foot nine but is a seven-footer because of long arms and big hands. That hurt Joe. Then he and Tank were somewhat similar—Tank was a bit better—and they were both still relatively young. Joe became a reserve, and that made him a disappointment because of where he was drafted.

Looking back, we should have drafted Karl Malone, but realistically, many other teams passed on him, too. No one could honestly say at the time that he knew how good Karl was going to be. Both Chris Mullin and Detlef Schrempf were available—Joe was the sixth pick, and those guys went in the next two spots—and we needed another small forward type. We had given up a future first-round pick to get Terry Tyler. As for Malone, we already had a good young power forward in Otis; and few people thought that Karl would ever be as good as Otis Thorpe was at the time. Until Chris Webber came along, Otis was the best power forward the Sacramento Kings ever had.

The glue that held everything together was Billy Jones, our trainer, who passed away last spring. If there's such a thing as a hall of fame trainer, he's the guy in every sense. I knew he was special then, but I didn't know how special until years later when I looked back at all the things he was responsible for—not only the training duties, but also travel arrangements back when we flew commercial and a hundred other things. Now we have two or three people doing those jobs. With Jonesy's personality, the players liked and respected him so much that he was able to get them to help him with the luggage and things like that. I'm not sure that anyone could accomplish that today. Working alone, he took care of travel, took care of luggage, and took care of the players, coaches, and media. He was just a bundle of energy, a one-in-a-million human being, and his legacy is that he hired Pete Youngman as his replacement. If there was a no. 1 guy to come through that franchise in the last 20 years, it would probably be Jonesy.

We had what we called "The Jonesy Rule:" If you can't get along with Jonesy, we don't need you. That rule was absolutely 100 percent accurate. If a player, or coach, or whoever couldn't get along with Jonesy, they had problems that needed severe counseling—simple as that. You didn't need to mess with them on your team. We didn't have anyone who broke the rule that first season. The second season was a different story.

Joe Kleine protects the paint. *Mike Powell/NBAE/Getty Images*

CHAPTER SIX

Mr. Smith Goes to Sacramento

L ooking back at it now, it seems silly, but we faced some pressure to make the playoffs that first year. We struggled early, and I know Phil Johnson was feeling some heat from the front office. Gregg Lukenbill and Joe Axelson were worried that we'd lose the fan support if we didn't start winning. They thought the fans would turn on the team, the way they do in most other cities. Well, we know now that that wasn't going to happen. We had a 10-year honeymoon period, pretty much, and we could have completely rebuilt the team the first couple of years and lost 60 games a year without driving away the fans.

In order to try to make the 1986 playoffs, Phil made what I thought was a gutsy move: He overhauled the starting lineup toward the latter part of the season. He decided to bring Drew off the bench, and he started Woody and Reggie, two bigger guards. He changed the front line, too, starting Terry Tyler and Olberding at forward and bringing Eddie Johnson and Thorpe off the bench. Did Phil have an epiphany of some sort? We were losing, and the coaching staff was trying to find some way to get an advantage. I think that's how epiphanies happen: You're struggling to find something that works better. Necessity is the mother of epiphany. We started playing better, whether it was the lineup change or not. Our guys came together. You never really know how that happens. Sometimes more can be made of the coaching and chemistry issues than should be. Let the players go, learn to execute the plays more efficiently, learn their roles—hopefully, it works by itself.

The result of the big change was that we played better basketball most nights when the starters sat down, and we went to our reserves. If our starters could just hang in there until the reserves went in, we were okay. I'm sure many people have forgotten that we didn't just sneak into the playoffs—we ended up seventh in the Western Conference. However, making the playoffs proved a good news and bad news situation. First off, we weren't going anywhere. We were swept in three games in the first round by Houston, which had Hakeem Olajuwon and Ralph Sampson. Second, finishing strong maybe gave us some delusions of grandeur.

The front office decided that we could make a trade or two because we were smarter than everyone else, and then we'd become a championship team. To me, it was a case of people getting a little greedy. Obviously, we didn't need to do anything spectacular. The team was getting better. The guys liked each other and won over the fans. We only had one guy, Mark Olberding, who was at the end of his career. We would have been a 40- to 45-win team for years to come if we had drafted someone each year and maybe made a minor move here and there. Instead, we broke up a playoff team.

The big move in the first season was acquiring Terry Tyler. We'd struggled and didn't have a backup small forward. Terry was a free agent. Joe Axleson signed him, and in order to ensure Detroit didn't match, we flip-flopped draft picks with the Pistons—we could have had the ninth or 10th pick instead of the 17th. Jack McCloskey, who was the Pistons' GM at the time, told me several years later Detroit wouldn't have matched the contract we gave Terry anyway. We ended up taking Harold Pressley with that 17th pick. Whether we could have chosen someone better with our original pick, I don't know. We could have taken Scott Skiles or Dennis Rodman where we chose Harold. I only bring this up to point out that, while Terry certainly helped us that first season, there was no good reason to think we'd be successful swinging for the fences with another trade.

So what did we do? We swung for the fences and whiffed. We sent Woody, Drew, and our first-round pick to the Clippers for the late Derek Smith, Franklin Edwards, and Junior Bridgeman. Actually, we had signed Derek and Franklin—who were restricted free agents—to offer sheets, but Los Angeles matched, so we ended up making a trade. As the years went by, people learned that the Clippers had no intention of matching our offers—just like the Pistons had no intention of matching our offer to Tyler—because they thought Derek was damaged goods. But in order to prevent them from matching, we ended up giving away some good players and what turned out to be the third pick in the draft. The Clippers took Charles Smith with that pick. He wasn't a major star, but he definitely was a solid forward. Even if we had made the trade and kept that lottery pick—L.A. certainly would have gone for that deal, in hindsight—we'd have been much better off.

We never discussed the trade as a coaching staff until after it had been decided. I don't know how much Phil Johnson was involved. I got the impression that he was aware of it, but it certainly wasn't his decision. Phil was a good soldier, so he didn't complain about it too much. If he'd have known what was coming, he might have reacted differently.

Any way you slice it, the trade was bad. You often see that around the league now with new owners who don't really understand how the league works. They get ahead of themselves in trying to push their teams to the next level. Making this trade set our franchise back four, five, six years—who knows? Derek wasn't able to play at a high level, and he ultimately became a real distraction. A team that had great chemistry and made the playoffs became a team that had very poor chemistry the next season.

If Derek hadn't played so well against us the previous season, I doubt we'd have made the deal. He looked like a star at times when he was with the Clippers, especially against us. He was a guy you thought could be a major player—maybe not the kind to bring you a championship, but a Mitch Richmond kind of star-type player. The bad news was that he had major knee surgery that year, and one important question remained unanswered: Was he ever going to get back to 100 percent? Hindsight is easy, of course, but he only showed a few star-like flashes after the surgery.

Neither of the other two players we received from Los Angeles was a factor, either. Junior never played for us. He was a good guy and had a good career, but he didn't have anything left. Franklin really didn't play much the next two years due to injuries. Had he stayed healthy, he would have been a good backup for us. When he played, he was fine. But he didn't play enough to make a difference, so the deal had no silver lining.

The chemistry issue was apparent immediately because Mike Woodson was a guy everyone thought the world of, and Larry was well liked, too. Could the trade have worked? Sure: We still had a good group of guys and decent talent—Reggie, Otis, and Eddie all averaged more than 18 points—so if Derek could have come in and been a star, we could have been okay even though he wasn't anything like Woody personality-wise. Derek's declining abilities led to frustration that permeated the locker room, making the players miss Woody and Drew even more.

I don't want to speak ill of the deceased, but Derek was a downer in many ways. Much was expected of him because of his big contract and the guys we gave up, and he simply couldn't produce. So he turned on the coaches, trainers, teammates, media … everybody. He wasn't happy here, didn't like it here; and quite honestly, nobody liked him, either. Having Derek on the team certainly took the fun out of it, because our first group of guys was so good to be around, and Derek certainly wasn't.

Of course, the guy who took the fall when things didn't work out was Phil. The team didn't play nearly as well because of chemistry issues and because it didn't have nearly as much talent. Phil was fired for that, which is kind of the way it always plays out. Really, it also cost Joe Axelson his job later. That trade tarnished Joe, which is unfortunate, because it led to some other poor decisions by the club down the line. The Kings were kind of like a house of cards—one really major bad move ultimately led to several other things changing in the organization. I think it even affected how Gregg Lukenbill looked at being an owner—the pizzazz was gone for him.

Speaking of losing your pizzazz, February 2, 1987, is a date that will live in infamy for me. We were only 14-31 at the time, and we had to go into Los Angeles and play one of the greatest teams of all time. We didn't make a shot from the floor in the first quarter and scored only four lousy points on free throws. The Lakers led 40-4 after 12 minutes. Before our next game, Phil and Frank Hamblen had been fired, and guess who was named interim coach?

I think Phil was feeling some pressure at the time, but I don't believe he knew how thin the ice was. We all felt that the team had overachieved the year before, and so we thought Phil had a little more leeway. I was shocked when he was fired, especially because so much was made of that first-quarter performance against L.A. I realize it's an embarrassment to only score four points, but the truth is, we outscored them the rest of the game. It's not as if the team had quit on Phil. We just had a bad quarter. Eddie missed some shots he usually made in his sleep. Besides that, the Lakers were better than us. They were better than everybody.

I just thought it was unfair the way it played out all the way around. We were playing poorly mainly because of a terrible trade. Was Phil going to win with that team? No, he wasn't—not with the guys that he had at that time. Of course, Red Auerbach wouldn't have won many games with that group, either.

Seeing Phil and Frank fired was difficult for me. When Joe Axelson first talked to me about taking the job, I called Phil to get his thoughts. He said, "You have to do it." We talked about the circumstances. He was very supportive in that regard. Now, I think he was certainly hurt to be fired, and I think at some point he may have had ideas that I had something to do with it, which is a perfectly normal thing. I think he and Frank both thought maybe I was working against them behind the scenes, but I was no Benedict Arnold. They know that now. But there was some resentment, which is just the way it works. Last season, Cleveland fired Paul Silas and named Brendan Malone the interim coach. I'm sure Brendan probably had many of the same mixed emotions I did. I'm sure Paul knows Brendan Malone didn't have squat to do with it, but there probably was a minute or two there when Paul was upset with him.

I asked Joe Axelson to please reconsider firing Phil because Phil was a good coach—better than me—and told him that it would be better to leave it as it was and stay with it. What I didn't know was that they not only had decided to fire Phil, but also to bring in a big name to replace him the following season. So it had nothing to do with me and my obvious basketball genius. They didn't see some brilliant coach in the making. They just said, "Well, we can put this young stiff out there, and he'll take one for the old club."

So that's how I went from being head coach at Pittsburg State in Kansas to one of the head coaching jobs in the most elite basketball league in the world within a year and a half. It was an amazing situation. I really didn't feel like I was prepared. I felt like in time I could be a good head coach in the league, but not right then. Honestly, I thought—and it turned out that I was right—taking the job would probably deprive me of a fair chance to be a head coach for the long term. In another couple of years as an assistant for Phil or someone else, I could have learned what I needed to learn and been in a better position to have success. But that choice wasn't there.

For most guys who aspire to be NBA coaches, it's a Catch-22 situation. There are only so many job openings, and when they come up, you simply can't afford to turn the opportunity down. But most people aren't Phil Jackson. They can't step into a ready-made situation. They get chances with lottery teams, with teams that have fired their coach because they're struggling, and when they don't turn them around in a year or two—oftentimes less—they're fired and end up with a nasty-looking record on their resume.

When I got my chance, the Kings' situation wasn't one I would have chosen for myself at all, and it really didn't serve my career well—at least as far as coaching goes. It was an impossible situation, similar to what we saw last season with Kevin Pritchard in Portland. He may never get the chance to be a head coach in the NBA again. Maybe he doesn't want to be one—but if he ever does, well … good luck. And Mike Woodson's going to have a heck of a time going somewhere after Atlanta unless they show a tremendous amount of patience with him, which they should. But will they? Probably not. History proves that once you have a big losing season, it's going to be tough to get out of that hole.

Coaching, or dancing to "Whatever Works"? *Otto Greule Jr./NBAE/Getty Images*

I never tried to position myself for the head-coaching job with the Kings. I said, "Well, that's not my decision to make," and I didn't worry about it. I think people will be surprised, but I didn't really want it. I was thrown into it. The Kings offered me a job for the following season, regardless of what I did as a coach. They gave me a raise that took my salary from $40,000 to $55,000 the next year plus $50,000 to finish out the term as the head coach, which was significant to me. Today, interim guys get a million bucks or something. I brought in Don Buse to be my assistant coach. The first game, I didn't have anyone with me on the bench. Don, who was from Holland, Indiana, and had been a very good player in the old American Basketball Association and the NBA, was very helpful.

Quite honestly—nobody's told me this—I'm convinced the Kings had every intention of firing me at the end of the year and paying me off. I don't think there was any intention to bring me back, unless it was to sell popcorn or take tickets. I tricked them, though, which makes me a little proud. The team performed a bit better after the coaching change. The fans in Sacramento really got behind me, which I truly appreciated. I think they realized that I was in an impossible situation. I was a real underdog, and people seemed to think that under the circumstances, we made the best of the situation. So the Kings kind of felt obligated to keep me around in some capacity to mollify the fans and the media.

Even around the league, many people were pulling for me. I remember Bill Fitch, who was coaching Houston at the time, telling me that he felt I was the rare interim coach who had actually made a difference and that the team was playing significantly better—more together—at the end of the year. That really meant a lot to me.

Honestly, one of the reasons we got better was that Derek quit playing the last two months due to injuries. We went 9-5 to end the season and only lost once by as many as 10 points. I wasn't surprised: I knew that once we didn't have to play Derek and put up with him, we'd get better. It was a clear case of addition by subtraction. Still, we weren't very good.

One of the things I tried to do was open up the offense. My feeling was that one of Phil's strengths was his structured offense.

That wasn't necessarily one of my strengths, so I chose something I found more comfortable. I didn't know if we'd win much more, but I thought we'd have more fun. I said to myself, "Self, Reggie's going to be on the floor, and he wants the ball, so let's give him the ball and give him more opportunities." He was so smart and so talented, he'd find ways of doing things regardless of the offense, so I tried to make it work for him and see if he could help us. I really encouraged him and Eddie Johnson to shoot three-pointers, which they really hadn't done much. The three really wasn't much of a weapon for anyone in the league yet. We used a little bit of the passing game and just tried to outscore some people.

The difference was noticeable, and the players seemed to enjoy playing that way. I had good relationships with the better players. My theory is, you're always going to have five guys who love you, five who dislike you, and two who aren't sure—the trick is to bring those last two around to keep the peace in the locker room. I'm sure some of the guys thought they should have played more, but Eddie, Reggie, and Otis, probably had as solid a year statistically as they had throughout their careers. I remember at the end of the year that I got into a little argument with Otis's agent, who didn't think I used Otis enough.

"Wait a minute, he averaged 21 points and 10 rebounds once I took over," I said. "My guess is that may be the best he'll ever do. So we're going to him enough."

That was my first taste of the impossibility of satisfying agents, because they only see it one way—their players all should play 40 minutes and get 25 shots a game. They're like parents.

With Reggie, sometimes you had to remind him that he wasn't the only one who could do things. I had to keep telling him, "You have to look for Eddie Johnson more." One time near the end of the season, we were playing in San Antonio, which was maybe a little better than we were. We had a chance to win a close game, so I was coaching my little rear end off. On two straight possessions, I called a play for EJ to come off a double stack. Reggie was supposed to maneuver and get him the ball for a 15-to-18-footer. Reggie missed him. He didn't run the play. He went to the other side and either missed the shot or went to the wrong guy.

Otis Thorpe shoots from the wing. *Mike Powell/NBAE/Getty Images*

Finally, I called a timeout.

"Reggie, I want you to run this play." I said. "If you don't, I'm going to run out on the floor, and I'm going to punch you in the nose."

And he looked at me funny and said, "You little idiot, I'll beat the crap out of you."

"Reggie, I have no doubt you can beat me up. But what you need to know is that if you don't run the play like I tell you, I'm going to run out on the floor and punch you in your nose," I told him. "You can do whatever you want after that, but that's what I'm going to do. You have to run this play. If you get the ball to Eddie, we can win this ballgame."

So we called the play again, Reggie ran it, Eddie hit the shot, and we won the ballgame.

On the way to the locker room to talk to the guys, Eddie ran up to me, and he said, "Jerry, you've got to tell me. What were you going to do? Would you have really hit him?"

"Eddie, I was going to run out there and punch him," I said. "I swear."

"I knew it," he said. "I told everybody that you were crazy enough to do it."

I absolutely was, and I think Reggie knew it, too. He would have kicked my butt, but I wanted to win that game, and I thought running that play down the stretch was the best way to do it.

I thought the world of Reg, but sometimes you had to lay it on the line with him. Another time, Reg was upset with Eddie—they'd always get into it a little bit—and said, "Every time I throw the ball to Eddie, he shoots it."

"Okay, Reg, you're the point guard, right?" I asked. "Well, you have the ball, so if you don't want him to shoot it, don't throw it to him. But keep this in mind: If the game gets close, you might want to throw it to him."

"I think I've got you now," he said.

I didn't want to complicate it too much, so I told him, "It's your damned ball, so you run the club, and if you think he's shooting too much, I'll deal with it. But Eddie's a shooter. If he's open, he should shoot it. That's what he does."

Reggie Theus gets "in focus." *Mike Powell/NBAE/Getty Images*

Harold Pressley was a rookie that year. I really encouraged Harold to become a three-point shooter. He was just a floppy kind of player. What I mean by that is, he didn't have a real game—nothing to hang his hat on. For him to become effective and stay in the league, he had to develop a long-distance shot. He had a nice stroke from the free throw line. I told him to take that out to three-point range. He even had a week—maybe it was his second year—where he was the NBA player of the week, mainly because of his three-point shooting.

As a coach, you have to encourage people to do things that they don't think they can do. If you have a good free throw shot, you just get a little more leg into it, and you can become a good three-point shooter. That's what you do as a coach: try to utilize players' strengths but also try to find some things they don't have and develop them. You can always wish you have Magic Johnson and James Worthy, but if you don't, you try to get more out of the guys you have. In a nutshell, that's the big secret of coaching.

CHAPTER SEVEN

The Fuss About Russ

Shortly after our second season in Sacramento ended—we went 29-53—Joe Axelson took me out to lunch and told me what was going to happen: Bill Russell, the greatest winner of all time, was going to become the coach for the 1987-88 season. They had hired Russ—it turned out—during the all-star break the previous season and gave him a seven-year contract. Russ was no fool, though. He didn't want to take over that particular team in the middle of the year.

Joe asked me to be at the press conference to offer my support, and that was fine. Joe had always treated me well. I wasn't stunned necessarily when they hired Russ. The only thing that bothered me was that they simply didn't tell me the truth in the first place. I would have been fine with that decision. I still would have tried to do as good a job as I could have the rest of the season. As I said, I wasn't trying to get the job.

I met Russ for the first time at the press conference. To Russ at the time, I could have been Joe Fadoozle. I don't think he had any particular regard for me at all, but I was kind of thrust upon him, which bothered me, but I figured I'd try to find a way to be valuable and get along with him and stick it out. Then, within a week or so, Willis Reed was hired to be the top assistant coach. I didn't know how that was going to go at first, although it worked out. We were three happy campers—at least for a little while.

Honestly, it was well into the preseason before Russ and I developed any relationship. I generally ran part of practice at one end of the floor with Willis running part of practice at the other end while Bill went place to place to visit and give his thoughts. He came down to my end of the court and came over to me and said, "Coach, let me talk to you a minute."

He put his arm around me and said, "You're a good coach. I've been watching you. I like what you're doing."

"Well, thanks. I appreciate that," I said. "I guess that works out good, since I'm going to be working for you."

"I think it's going to work good," he said.

From that point on, he'd come into my office—Russ, Willis, and I had an office together for a while there until Russ decided that he needed his own space—and we'd visit and kid and have a good time.

Even though I'd felt a little deceived by the way that things were done, I couldn't complain too much. They redid my contract, made it even a little better to stay on, and I'm glad that I signed it. Most people won't believe this, but I enjoyed Russ. I ended up having a good relationship with him. He was hard to get to know. I don't think he said five words to me for about three months, then once he decided I was okay, I couldn't get him to shut up. I spent a ton of time listening to his old stories, and he had some great ones. I had to become cackle-proof, though. If you've ever seen Russ on TV, you know what I mean. He has a very loud and distinctive laugh, more like a cackle, and while he seems dour in public much of the time, he laughs a lot. If you're around it enough, it'll drive you nuts.

Willis is one of the best people I've ever known, probably the most down-to-earth superstar you could meet. You could see why he was a hall of fame player because of the kind of person he was, the kind of work ethic he had, and what he expected from himself and others. He had his trials and tribulations as a coach, but he's like many other guys who went into bad situations. When you get with teams that don't have good players, you're not going to win.

I wouldn't trade the experience I had that season for anything. Here I am, a former juco coach from Indiana hanging out with Bill Russell and Willis Reed. My God, I would have paid to be in that

The Three Rs—Reed, Russell, and Reynolds. *Courtesy of Maloof Sports & Entertainment, Sacramento Kings*

position. People talk about the bad old days, those miserable years. Well, yeah, there were some bad teams and some bad times, but from my standpoint, there were many interesting things that were more valuable in my life than whether we won another five games or something. From a professional standpoint, yeah, it's much better to be around a 50-win team than a 25-win team. From a personal standpoint, it was the opportunity of a lifetime. And there were upsides from a professional standpoint, too. I actually did learn some things from both those guys, and Russ allowed Willis and me some leeway. We didn't have a 17-man coaching staff as they do these days. Russ was the head coach, but Willis and I really had a ton of input. We worked with the players often, which I enjoyed. Once you get past the fact we weren't very good, that season was one of my career highlights.

Was Russ a great coach? I couldn't honestly say that. But I really do think if Bill had had the opportunity to be the general manager with the Maloof family—our current owners—in charge, he would have had the chance for serious success. He had a good feel for talent, and the players liked him and respected him.

One of the problems Russ had in Sacramento went back to the very day he was introduced as head coach. He made the statement that he wasn't going to be the coach who led the Kings to the play-offs but he *would* be the coach to lead them to the championship. So he set himself up for failure from the start. Did I buy into it? I felt and hoped that he would improve the situation. But it was a big mistake on his part to say what he said, and I'm sure he'd agree looking back. We probably should have strived to be significant before talking about championships. I knew we didn't have anything near a championship-caliber team, regardless of who was coaching.

Had Russ himself come out of retirement, we'd have had a much better chance, because even at 57 or 58 he was much quicker and more athletic than either Joe Kleine or LaSalle Thompson. Once, Russ was running Joe and Tank through a drill on how to defend the low box from side to side, and I was watching and just marveling at how quick he still was and his length. His arms seemed a foot longer than Joe's or LaSalle's.

They weren't quite getting it, and I told him, "Russ, you could help this team a lot more if you would just play."

He just cackled and said, "I don't think so."

As good a time as I had with Russ and as well as he treated me, there's no question that he was an enigma. At times, he was difficult to be around in some ways just because he was *Bill Russell.* You couldn't go anywhere without people knowing him and wanting a few minutes of his time. He wouldn't sign autographs, which offended some people. One of the things that always puzzled me was that Russ had a deep distrust of all media. Surprisingly, the guy who did media work—he was an analyst on network NBA games for years— would come back and avoid the media or treat them badly, which he sometimes did. Of course, many treated him the same way in response. Russ was so strange in that way. Of course, the fans wanted to hear more from Russ, and if he were more available to the media, it might have served him well. He was one of the all-time greats, but he really didn't use it to his advantage in Sacramento.

Russ was, as you might imagine, also a very competitive guy. Once, we drove to a pre-draft camp. Russ drove his own car, and Willis and I were following him. Russ was such a wild driver that every drive was a race to the finish. He'd be in traffic like Jeff Gordon, cutting guys off, missing other cars by inches while driving 90 miles an hour.

I told him once, "Russ, you have to slow down. I know we're going to get in a wreck, and we'll all be dead."

I could see the headline: "Bill Russell, Willis Reed, and some unknown killed."

If I was going to be in a car wreck, I wanted to be the most important person in the car.

Russ was hired in April. Two months later, we traded Eddie Johnson to Phoenix for Ed Pinckney—who along with Harold Pressley had been part of Villanova's upset of Georgetown for the 1985 NCAA championship—and a second-round draft pick. Pinckney wasn't a bad player, but he couldn't replace Eddie. Russ came to me and asked why Joe Axelson wanted to trade Eddie so bad. I wasn't sure whether it was because Joe didn't like the way Eddie played or because EJ had gotten an offer sheet from Cleveland that the Kings had to match. Russ said, "Joe is committed to getting rid of EJ," and he asked me how I felt about it. Well, I liked Eddie Johnson and told him so. My feeling was Russ wasn't committed to Ed Pinckney at all, but that's what Joe wanted to do, so we went along with it. Russ probably should have known more about the personnel when he arrived, but he didn't see that trade as being that big a deal. Willis liked Pinckney. He liked bigger guys and wanted more of a low-post presence. In some circumstances, it might have worked, but we missed EJ.

We received a player in another minor trade before the start of the season that many Kings fans may not remember, but I certainly do. We sent a second-round draft pick to New York for center Jawann Oldham. Talk about your strange dudes. The day after the trade—Willis really wanted him because he was a great athlete, quick off his feet, long, marvelous defender—he came into a meeting with the coaching staff wanting to talk about getting an extension on his contract.

"Well, it's a little early for that," Russ said. "You're going to have to prove a little more."

"I know I'm better than Patrick Ewing," he said. "I just haven't had the opportunity."

I know Russ, Willis, and I all rolled our eyes and thought, "Oh, boy, this is going to be a little different than we thought."

Jawann had a very unclear picture of his own talent. He wasn't a stiff, and he wasn't disagreeable. Probably his only real flaws were that he couldn't shoot the ball at all, and he just thought that he was better than he was.

I don't think anyone disliked Jawann, and he wasn't really a troublemaker or complainer, just a bit of a loner who had his own agenda. I will never forget what Franklin Edwards, a backup guard with a great sense of humor, told me one day as I was searching for Jawann: "You don't want to go where Jawann's gone. He comes back sometimes, but you may not."

I kind of knew what he meant. Jawann was a very bright guy, but eccentric. He could have been a terrific backup center for 12 or 15 years if he could have understood that's what he was best equipped to do. The fact he couldn't get there—it may have dawned on him when he played in the CBA later—caused him many problems.

There was a game in Dallas maybe 15 or 20 games into the season. We'd been blasted, and Russ was going to have a talk with players before the press entered the locker room. Everybody sat down, and I thought Russ made some good points. He was trying to just point out some things, not being belligerent or picking on anyone in particular. Jawann stood up, with his uniform and warmup top on, and walked into the shower. We knew for sure then that his elevator didn't go completely to the top.

Russ's first game as head coach was against Golden State. We beat the Warriors 134-106. We were running the floor and going crazy. Our first-round draft pick, Kenny Smith, really looked good. All of the sudden, we had high hopes. They didn't last very long. We won three of our next 18 games. Our style didn't necessarily fit our players. We wanted to run, but you have to run with some purpose, and we didn't seem to have any. Russ had taken Reggie Theus off the point to play Kenny, and Reggie didn't like that—rightly so, because he was better at it than Kenny was. Some of the guys didn't want to play in the roles they had. Willis resigned in late February to take the head-coaching job in New Jersey, leaving me and Bill. By then, the players had given up. Things were falling like dominoes.

Kenny Smith was a first-round pick.
Otto Greule Jr./NBAE/Getty Images

So there I was again. I took over as coach with the team 17-41 in early March of 1988. Joe Axelson and Gregg Lukenbill talked to me about being the interim coach again, and I said, "No, I'm not going to do that. That doesn't seem right." I told them I'd finish the year, but then I wanted a contract for a full year beyond that, and they agreed to it.

To Russ's credit, about the middle of the next year, he signed me to a three-year contract. I've always been very appreciative of Russ, because I know he didn't have to do that. He just thought it was the right thing to do. Joe and Luke didn't want to give me any job security. Russ told me, "You've kind of held this thing together." He thought there had been a rush to judgment on him, and whether that's true or not, he thought I deserved more time. Looking back, if Russ hadn't had done that for me, I'd have been out the door when things continued to stay bad. But he made it convenient for the Kings to keep me in the front office when they decided to get another coach.

Anyhow, we had a season to finish. The first thing I did was to call Phil Johnson and ask if he'd come back as my assistant coach. I don't know if that decision worked out very well—but it certainly wasn't Phil's fault. Although Phil was great about everything, both of us felt uncomfortable. The reason I brought him back, obviously, was that I felt I owed him, and I always will. But I also felt that he was the best guy I could hire. I knew he was an excellent coach. He was a loyal guy, a good friend, and he had been a good assistant as well as a head coach. Bringing him back made sense—he had been here and knew the players. But in my mind, the adjustment had to be difficult for him. He was a more experienced, more proven coach than I was—and having so much respect for Phil didn't make the situation any easier for me. We made the best of it, but we didn't have any miracle cures for what ailed the Kings.

We went 7-17 after Russ moved upstairs to finish the 1987-77 season 24-58. We were just too far gone at that point to turn things around, and we had some injury problems. At one point, we brought in a guy whose name has been buried in the sands of time; a guy who made Jawann Oldham look like Wilt Chamberlain or a young Russ: Martin Nessley was a seven-foot-two guy out of Duke who didn't really play much in college. The Clippers had him for a while early in the season. We were just desperate to pick up a big body late in the year, because LaSalle Thompson, who was about the most durable guy in the world, hurt his knee. As bad luck would have it, we got Martin. He was a very bright guy who saw what everyone else did wrong, but he couldn't spot some of the little flaws in his own game. We signed him to 10-day contract when he was sick in the hospital. We thought he'd be able to play, but he really couldn't. Not that he was going to contribute much on the court, but we needed a warm body, and he wasn't even really that. Then we signed him to a *second* 10-day contract—talk about desperation.

We held out hope that Derek Smith would come around for a while. Around the all-star break, I'd finally decided that was never going to happen.

You'd see Harold Pressley and other guys outplaying him in practice and say, "Why are we doing all this? Why are we running special plays for Derek and posting him up?"

Derek would say, "I need the ball here, and I can do this and that," but the fact was, he couldn't. He had been a decent post player, but he didn't have the same legs under him. We'd run plays for him and wouldn't get anything out of them. We had other guys who could score easier and better.

Of course, I was under some major pressure from the front office even then to play him because he was our highest paid guy.

"Yeah, well, okay," I said. "But I can see it isn't working and so do Derek's teammates."

Only in the NBA do you have situations sometimes where you play guys who aren't the best players for reasons that have nothing to do with basketball. In junior high school, you generally play the best players. In high school, you play the best players. In college, I always played the best players, not necessarily the guys I recruited the hardest or whatever. At some point, you say, "These are my best guys, and that's who I'm going to play."

But in the NBA, so many teams—it still applies—end up playing guys who don't deserve their time based on their abilities. They play them because of contracts or because the team drafted them or traded for them. The difference between good franchises and poor ones is that the good franchises make those decisions quicker. If they've made a mistake, they move on, whether it's drafts, trades, or whatever, and the bad ones refuse to believe it for much longer. We just kept taking one step forward and two steps back as an organization. It was a comedy of errors for us back then.

As a franchise, back in the day, we hung on to our mistakes way too long. That was one of our real flaws. Rather than just admit a mistake, we'd beat a dead horse. We tried to find ways to make things work. Look at Joe Kleine—he was a high draft pick, but it was obvious that he wasn't as good as LaSalle Thompson was. Well, that didn't mean Joe couldn't play, because he could, but LaSalle was better. At some point, we had to get past our mistaken expectations that Joe was going to be the savior at center and just figure out a way to get things done between the two of them. I was too young or inexperienced at the time to see all that. But as the years have gone by, you see other franchises and why they don't succeed, and you realize that the higher-ups are making decisions about trying to pound a square peg into a round hole. With the franchise we currently have—the ownership and leadership—it's so very different. That's one of the reasons we're better … aside from having better players.

Russ was one of those square peg–round hole deals. My feeling was that he was more interested in running a basketball team than in coaching. He had being GM in mind when he signed on with us, and coaching was just a way to get his foot in the door. I don't think he had any real love of coaching, and you need that to be successful. The coaching thing hurt him in the front office, too, because he was a little tarnished as far as everybody was concerned. Joe Axelson's status was changed, too, because Russ came in with more authority than Joe. Ultimately, Joe was fazed out of the organization.

Things continued to stay bad, so where do you go? As a front office person, Russ made some mistakes. People bring up taking Pervis Ellison with the first pick in the 1989 draft. Pervis turned out to be a mistake, but there were about 10 mistakes in the first round that year. Remember J.R. Reid, Stacey King, and George McCloud? It was just a bad draft—probably the best guy in the top 20 was Tim Hardaway, and he went 14th. But looking at the two drafts before that, he did pretty well.

Kenny Smith, our 1987 pick, had a solid career. Kenny was a little wild, a little out of control, and not a true point guard. He could be frustrating to watch. He was so fast and so agile that he'd get out in front of a fast break, make a beautiful move to get past the defender, and then miss the lay-up. He eventually became a good perimeter shooter even though he had a strange-looking shot. He was very likable, though, and he came to play. In his second year, Kenny was playing about 40 minutes a game, and every time I took him out he'd get mad at me. He'd say: "I want to play." I'd tell him, "I understand, but you're playing more than anyone else." I'd explain it to him every game, and the next game I'd take him out to rest for two minutes, and he'd be glaring at me. But that's one of the reasons he was a good player. He never wanted to come off the court. Kenny ended up making the all-rookie team.

After the season, Russ made a controversial trade that ended up—for one season, at least—looking smart. He sent Reggie Theus to Atlanta for the 18th pick in the 1988 draft and Randy Wittman.

Reggie and LaSalle Thompson were the last of the Mohicans from the team that moved to Sacramento. Russ told me about the deal, and I asked if I could talk to Reggie first to see if he wanted to go to Atlanta. I felt we owed him that much. Reggie thought it over and decided that the move would be good for him. The Hawks had Dominique Wilkins and Moses Malone, so they had championship aspirations—that didn't work out, of course. The Hawks were still a very good team, and they were taking a chance because Randy had been a great fit for them. He was a fit-in guy, and obviously we needed more than that. He didn't have a very good career here, but he was part of a later trade that helped us get Wayman Tisdale.

We took Vinny Del Negro with our own second-round pick in the '88 draft, and he proved to be a very good choice. With that pick from Atlanta, we drafted a player who had all the earmarks of being a star whom we could begin to rebuild around—Ricky Berry.

Vinny Del Negro brings the ball up the court.
Otto Greule Jr./NBAE/Getty Images

CHAPTER EIGHT

Collapse

The only season in which I was the Kings' coach from start to finish was 1988-89. Although I felt prepared, I didn't have too many illusions. I don't think anyone went into the year thinking we'd be strong—maybe that we'd be a bit better, but that's it. I knew we had many weaknesses. For example—this is something fans of the recent vintage of Kings teams will understand—we weren't very athletic.

Still, there were some reasons to be moderately excited. For one thing, we finally moved into the much-larger Arco Arena II after three years in the temporary facility. Arco II is taking its hits now, but we were thrilled. When I first joined the Kings, The Forum in Los Angeles was considered the best building in the league, although it didn't compare to the arenas these days—no luxury suites, it wasn't in a great part of L.A., and you couldn't get sushi at the concession stands. I think Gregg Lukenbill wanted a building more impressive than The Forum, and Arco II certainly was the best arena in California when it opened. We might have lost a little bit of the home-court advantage we'd had in the first arena. Even with 7,000 more fans involved, the atmosphere wasn't as crazy at it had been—the first arena was rocking every single night.

We also had a new look on the floor. We had drafted Ricky Berry and Vinny Del Negro, and they'd be helpful—though maybe not right away, certainly down the line. Just about a month before the season, we sent Otis Thorpe to Houston for Rodney McCray and Jim Peterson. We planned to get two potential starters for one, and I guess it worked out okay. Jim was a role player. Rodney was one of the better all-around players we've had until recently.

Looking back, we gave Otis a big contact in order to do a sign-and-trade deal with Houston. Would we have been better off just keeping Otis, even with the big contract? There's not any doubt in my mind about that. Otis was a star at his position, maybe the fifth or sixth best power forward in the league. People—especially fans who call sports talk shows with ideas about trades—become confused about how important talent is in the NBA. If you trade a legitimate top player, no amount of mediocre players you receive can make up for him. Basketball's a game where one truly gifted player can make a tremendous difference. We traded Otis when he was healthy and in his prime, so it wasn't like sending Chris Webber to Philadelphia. As good as Rodney was—as things went forward—Otis had the better career. The trade was purely financial, and those kinds of trades hurt this franchise. I understand the owner's position: Money was a problem; but it was very difficult to compete with teams where money wasn't a problem.

Rodney was very quiet, tough, and competitive. His biggest drawback was that he was a spotty shooter. I always thought, as the years went on, that if Rodney had made the commitment, he would have been a much better power forward than small forward. But he didn't really want to play the position at least at the time we got him. He was an excellent defensive rebounder in terms of rebounds per minute and coming out of a crowd with the ball; and he could guard most threes and fours in the league. He would have been excellent in today's game because of his ability to play all-court. In many ways, he's just the kind of player the Kings needed last season.

I had a few problems with Rodney early. He didn't want to be traded to Sacramento. He was happy in Houston. He won an NCAA championship at Louisville; he was the third selection in the draft; and he had gone to the NBA Finals with the Rockets. The fact

Rodney McCray gets into non-smile mode. *Stephen Dunn/NBAE/Getty Images*

that Houston decided to trade him was a blow to Rodney, and it took him a while to get over that. I didn't know what to do about Rodney. He was playing okay, but the team was struggling, and I wanted him to step up even more. I just couldn't get through to him. He wouldn't pay attention to me. I don't know if it was really true or just my perception. He probably heard everything I said, but he wouldn't respond—like talking to your wife when she's mad at you.

One game, I finally went berserk in the locker room. At half-time, I went over to Rodney's locker, next to Jim Petersen. Rodney was there, but I didn't even look at him.

"I'm going to talk to Rodney McCray's locker because I want to be able to communicate with something in this vicinity," I said. "So locker, let me explain to you what I would like to get out of Rodney McCray."

I talked to the locker for quite a while there and got it out of my system. I probably used some profanity, but I had a good conversation with the locker.

"I realize you won't talk back or respond to me, but Rodney doesn't either," I said. "And I want to get my point across to you."

Rodney looked at me funny, probably thinking, "This guy is a whack job."

But Jim told me afterwards, "You'll never have problems with Rodney again. He really liked that."

Jim was right. From that point on, I could kid Rodney, have fun with him, and talk to him.

If we had any reason to be optimistic at the start of the season, it didn't last long. We opened 0-7, including a 40-point loss at Dallas and a 30-point loss at home against Phoenix. We were 3-14 when my assistant coach, Phil Johnson, was offered the chance to go to Utah as Jerry Sloan's top assistant. I knew the Jazz was going to be a good team, and our future wasn't very bright, so I had no problems with letting Phil go. I could see the odds of us being a winner any-time soon weren't very good, so if Phil stayed, we both might have been fired at any time.

That's the way the league is—it inevitably comes down to the coach. It was a good break for Phil, and he helped that team. I'm proud that we let him go, because we didn't have to, and most teams and coaches wouldn't have approved that in the middle of the season. I really, truly felt it was the best thing for Phil. Of course, it's also true that his presence wasn't going to be the difference between 55 and 60 wins for us. Phil's a good coach, but not that good.

I needed an assistant coach, so we brought in the late Herman Kull. He had been scouting for us, so he knew the system and the players. Herman was a very bright basketball guy. He came out of New Jersey with what they called the "five-star group:" Mike Fratello, Richie Adubato, Hubie Brown, Brendan Suhr, and Herman. Unfortunately, Herman was the least personable of the group, which hurt his career. He'd been an assistant with George Karl at Golden State and worked for Adubato in Detroit, so he had the NBA experience.

Herman tended to be cynical and negative. Rodney McCray told me once, "Usually the head coach is kind of the bad guy, and the assistant coach gets to be the good guy. It's a total flip-flop here."

At one point, Bill Jones, our trainer, and I told Herman that we weren't going to let him eat with us anymore if he didn't stop sending food back to the kitchen. Every meal, something was undercooked or overcooked or whatever—it took the fun out of eating. Now, Herman had some good ideas as far as strategy went, and the fact the team was bad certainly wasn't his fault, but he was a piece of work.

We went into Washington for a game, and the Bullets—as they were called at the time—had a notorious heckler who sat right behind the visiting bench. The guy's name was Robin Ficker. He never used profanity, but he was extremely loud and obnoxious and came up with some great put-downs. I was amazed that an apparently intelligent person could be so obnoxious, but he busted the whole team up by getting on Herman.

I took a timeout in the third quarter, and he yelled, "Reynolds! Jerry Reynolds! Reynolds! Let me ask you a question: How long did it take you to find him?"

I looked up at Ficker because I had no idea what he was talking about, and he yelled, "How long did it take you to find an assistant coach who's smaller and uglier than you are?"

All the players looked at Herman—you could see he was seething—and just lost it. After he stopped laughing, Rodney said, "Hey, it's true."

"I ain't a pretty man," I told Herman. "But I look pretty good compared to you."

The guy I really wanted to hire for that job was Don Buse, who'd been my assistant the first time I was named interim head coach. He had decided to get away from the NBA and pursue other interests, though. A few years later, Jerry Krause, who was the Bulls' general manager, called me. He wanted to hire Don as an assistant coach for Doug Collins and was looking for some opinions. I told him that he couldn't hire a better guy than Buse. But Don really didn't want to do it—he was raising horses and was happy with his life. So the Bulls ended up hiring a guy named Phil Jackson. I wonder how that turned out.

Maybe the lowest point of that season came on December 27. We were coming off four straight road losses and playing a very good Portland team at home. I'd been on a diet, and I hadn't been sleeping well because of the team, the travel, and the pressure of the job. During the game, my habit was to squat down, because I didn't want to block the view of the folks in the expensive seats. I had a tendency to be a bit animated—jumping up and down, making a fool of myself, whatever. In a few games before that one, I'd felt a little dizziness during the game, so I'd just go sit down and be okay. I was probably like most men in America: If it goes away, everything's fine.

We were ahead of Portland most of the way. In the third quarter, I thought Joe Kleine was fouled at the other end of the floor (my eyesight was really keen when I was coaching). I jumped up, yelled something, and ran toward mid-court.

All of the sudden I started seeing green squiggly things in front of my eyes. I said to myself, "Self, you need to sit down somewhere."

So I turned to head back to the bench, and that's the last I remember until I saw Jonesy getting ready to give me some mouth-to-mouth resuscitation. I remember thinking, "Death would be preferable." Then about half of section 105 was hovering around me—everybody who had any kind of professional title. There were a couple of barbers, some dentists, a real estate agent, a few car sales-men, a proctologist, maybe even some people who actually might have been able to help … everyone was there.

I didn't feel terrible. I mean, I didn't feel good, but I didn't feel like I'd had a heart attack because my chest wasn't hurting. That was the first thing I thought about. Of course, the doctors wanted to be careful about that, so they carted me off. One of the referees, Blaine Reichelt, had called a technical foul on me. He knew I could be kind of a jerk and thought I might have been goofing around by falling down. When he realized it was for real, he rescinded the technical. Mike Schuler, who's a good friend of mine, was coaching Portland, and he was mad that they didn't get the free throw. I always kid him, "You didn't care about me. You just wanted that point." As it turned out, Harold Pressley hit a shot at the buzzer to win the game by a point. Of course, if they'd had the technical, it might have gone into overtime—and the way things were going, we'd have probably lost.

Not too long after that game, the Blazers let Mike go. I always told him, "I went to a lot of trouble to get you fired." Over the years, about 400,000 people have told me that they were at that game. To this day, I'll have people come up and ask me about my health, whether my heart's good. I used to try to explain what actually hap-pened—I just blacked out because of a dizzy spell. Now I just say, "Everything's great since I had the transplant."

About a month later, things came to a head with Derek Smith. Derek was just more of the same: He couldn't play because of this injury or that, and when he did play, he said we weren't using him right. The same thing that happened to Phil was happening to me, so finally we got into it in Milwaukee, and I had to suspend him.

I called our owner, Gregg Lukenbill, and said, "It's kind of at the point where if you want that guy on the team, you really need to get somebody else to coach. We have better players than Derek who aren't playing because of him, especially Ricky Berry and Harold Pressley. They're not getting enough time because we're trying to sal-vage the unsalvageable."

I've always respected Gregg, because he said, "You're right, we've tried everything, and we've been patient enough."

We ended up waiving Derek within a few days of the suspension.

The very first game that Ricky started in place of Derek, we beat Golden State 142-117 and set an NBA record with 16 three-pointers. Ricky hit seven of them and scored 35 points. Vinny Del Negro had four or five three-pointers. It was interesting: The three-point record was a big deal as long as New York had it. The Knicks had 12, and that stood as the record for a long time. But then we shattered it and went on to get 12 in a couple of other games, and suddenly it wasn't a big deal. It was like, "Ah, well, it's on the West Coast, so it doesn't mean anything now."

We shot a ton of threes out of necessity. We didn't really have a low-post game or true center. We tried to spread the floor, draw, and kick to use our deep shooters, and we gave players the green light to shoot threes in transition if they had a good look, as many teams do now. We were probably a little ahead of the curve on that.

Incidentally, the night we suspended Derek, we ended up being more than one player shorthanded, because Larry Krystkowiak of the Bucks splattered Jim Peterson's nose all over his face with one of the most vicious punches I've ever seen. It was the third quarter, and Krystkowiak just turned and popped him. Jim was KO'd on the floor.

I ran out there, and when Jim came to, he said, "Coach, I'm okay. I think I can play."

"Jim, unless you can breathe out of your ears, I don't think you can." I said.

His nose was sideways and flattened. He and Krystkowiak, who's now the head coach at the University of Montana, were good friends, too. Jim even said that he'd brought it on him himself. He'd been pinching him, poking him, pulling the hair on his legs—just messing with him—and Larry told him that he was going to smack him if he didn't stop. The short right hand of Krystkowiak's was on EPSN for a week. Every player in the league saw that, and from that point on, Krystkowiak had free sailing in the NBA.

I always thought Joe Kleine could have done the same thing, flattened someone and gotten a reputation as a tough guy. Joe's one of the nicest guys you'd want to meet, but being a bully just once might have served his career well. He tried it one time after he left us. He got into it with Mark Bryant of Portland. It was comical. They both had enormous heads. Well, they got their big noggins together, and they were trying to hit each other, but with those two melons in the way, neither could get a clear shot.

Bill Russell completely changed the look of the team with two huge trades in a four-day span after the All-Star Game. We sent LaSalle Thompson and Randy Wittman to Indiana for power forward Wayman Tisdale, then got guard Danny Ainge and backup center Brad Lohaus from Boston for Kleine and Ed Pinckney.

Unlike Rodney McCray, Danny had a good attitude about coming to Sacramento. He had been part of two championship teams in Boston and he saw that with Larry Bird, Kevin McHale, Robert Parrish, and Dennis Johnson, he'd never be paid what he'd like to be paid. I think he was right. Russ had told me before he made the deal that Danny was ready to try something different. With the Kings, he sure got something different.

Danny was the coach on the floor … and off the floor, on the bus, in the airport terminal, wherever. Most people disliked him. He was known as the guy who bit Tree Rollins during a fight, even though Tree did the biting. Danny had a reputation as a whiner and complainer. Part of that was just because most people hated the Celtics. I knew he was very good, but I didn't know how good he was until we got him. I know Russ was confident that Danny was going to make us better, which he did, and not just with his talent but with his passion for the game and his leadership.

One game in Seattle, we were ahead at the half even though the Sonics were a much better team than we were, and I was trying to come up with something motivational at halftime.

"Guys, you're going to have to imagine that you're a quality team," I said. "You are the Chicago Bulls; you are the Cleveland Cavaliers. Just imagine that you're of that caliber, and you can beat the Sonics because you're better. Just visualize that, and you'll beat these guys."

We came out of the third quarter ahead a few points. We went through most of the fourth quarter ahead, then in the last three or four minutes we collapsed as usual, and the Sonics beat us. I was walking off the floor down in the dumps, and Danny came up, put

The late Ricky Berry was a rookie star. *Tim DeFrisco/NBAE/Getty Images*

Danny Ainge strategizes with Herman Kull.
Ken Levine/NBAE/Getty Images

his arm around me and said, "Coach, shake it off. Just visualize that we won."

That was Danny. He always had a way of keeping things in perspective. Most people might have taken what he said that time the wrong way, but he wasn't being a jerk or anything. The thing about Danny was that he always gave a great effort and didn't have one ounce of choke in him. I'd rather have a guy who could give a great effort, shake it off if we came up short, and then be ready to compete the next time than some guy who didn't really care but pretended to be really hurt after each loss.

Danny had an opinion about everything, and I kicked him out of a couple of practices. But there was never a day I didn't like him, and we got along well. The way he is—his stubbornness and single-mindedness—explains the success he's had.

Late in the season, Danny came up to me and said, "Coach, I've been thinking a lot about our team, and I think I know what our problem is."

"Danny, please share that with me. I think I have a pretty good idea myself, but I'd be interested in your thoughts, too."

"Well, I'm your best player."

"Yeah, you certainly are," I said.

"If I'm your best player," he told me, "we're going to have a tough time winning. I was about the fifth-best player in Boston, and I'm probably not quite as good now."

It was funny, but at the same time, he was exactly right. Danny had a knack for seeing things as they were, whereas most players see things as they wish they were.

Most Kings fans, I think, have forgotten how good Danny was. When you look at those early years, the most gifted all-around player we had was Reggie Theus. Danny shouldn't have been as good as Reggie was, but he was better—a little better athlete with a more consistent competitive fire about him. I know Mitch Richmond was the MVP of an All-Star Game, but Danny was a better all-around player because he consistently made his teammates better. Really, he was our point guard, and Kenny Smith was the shooting guard, which worked great for us, because no big guard in the league could keep Danny from getting the ball where he needed to get it. It worked well, and I'm surprised more teams don't play that way. Not that it was any great genius—we did it because we had no choice. Kenny was so erratic as a ball-handler.

Danny averaged a tick over 20 points in his games with us that season, and Wayman Tisdale scored a tick under 20. Tizzie was a very personable guy who had been the second overall pick in the draft behind Patrick Ewing. He'd been something of a disappointment at Indiana. He was an undersized power forward, but he brought us a little bit of a low-post presence. He could really score the ball with his little half-hook, which came to be known as the "Tizzie flip." He helped our transition game because we'd just run him to the block and try to get him the ball before he was double-teamed. He was a poor passer out of the double team because he was relatively small. He couldn't see over it. Even guards could help and give him trouble. Plus, he was so one-handed. He wouldn't have noticed if his right arm was chopped off at the shoulder—at least when it came to basketball. I imagine he needs it to play the bass. He's become a very accomplished musician since he retired. LaSalle Thompson had been very popular here, but trading him for Tizzie was a good trade for both teams, one of the few that worked out well for us back in those days.

We ended up 27-55 that season. Going in, I had no preconceived notion about how many we'd win, and given what had gone on during the season—the turmoil with Derek, the trades, and all that—I can't say I was terribly surprised or even disappointed with the record. Our roster included players like Randy Allen, Ben Gillery, and Michael Jackson. Once they left our franchise, they were out of the league, never to be heard from again, which is a good clue that your roster isn't really up to NBA standards. That was always a problem with our team back in those weak years. You look at the top five or six guys, and they were good players, but the rest of the roster largely was marginal talent. Through the season, you always have injuries, and that's what would kick you in the butt. A Randy Allen or somebody has to play big minutes all of the sudden. Brad Lohaus certainly belonged in the NBA, but if he has to be a 35-minute guy, or if Michael Jackson is your third guard and has to play 20-25 minutes, you're weak.

I'll say this, though: I went into every game thinking we could win. I don't know if that's a character flaw or what. Logic would tell you that's not the best way to look at it. We might be in a long losing streak, but by the next game, I'd think, "We can win this one." I figured that we'd find a way. Maybe it was just a matter of the other team playing beneath their ability. If we hadn't had gotten Wayman and Danny, maybe the record wouldn't have been much different, but certainly the way we were playing at the end of the season would have been. We never would have been competitive with that original cast—we just couldn't score enough.

However, things were improving steadily. We'd had to adjust on the fly after the trades, which cost us some games, but we played .500 basketball the last month of the season as things came together. Kenny and Danny really clicked together in the backcourt—and

Wayman Tisdale slams it home. *Otto Greule Jr./NBAE/Getty Images*

with Tisdale and Ricky Berry, we were decent at every position except center. We lucked out and got the number-one pick in the draft. What could go wrong?

CHAPTER NINE

The Matter
of Motta

Two major problems, generally speaking, existed with the Kings in the early years. We had no real leadership, and we caught bad breaks. Two of the worst breaks came in 1989.

First, we owned the first pick in the draft in a year when there really wasn't anyone worth taking number one. The other break—one much more devastating to the team's productivity, morale, and future—was the suicide of Ricky Berry. Only a few months after a rookie season in which he'd averaged 11 points and three rebounds per game, Ricky shot himself on August 14.

Ricky's suicide and the drafting of Pervis Ellison created a double whammy. Quite honestly, if those two things went differently—if there was a good player to take first overall and Ricky didn't commit suicide—the Kings were a team that probably could start winning again. Instead, we had the worst season of the franchise's Sacramento era.

I think Ricky would have been very similar to Dale Ellis. He would have been a 20-point scorer for many years. Ricky probably shot the ball deep as easily as Ellis or Peja Stojakovic—maybe he wasn't as consistent as those guys from the outside, but Ricky had more ability going to the basket. He was quicker and more athletic than either of them, and if a defender tried to take away the outside shot, Ricky would have gone right around him. Whether Ricky would have scored 20 or 25 points per game, I don't know. The only question in my mind was how many times he'd make the all-star team.

Losing Ricky was sadly similar to Boston losing Len Bias—the Celtics' transition from the Larry Bird-Kevin McHale era was denied them as a franchise, and when their stars retired, they were done. The impact that Ricky's suicide had on the Kings is one of those things that you can never measure—quite honestly, it's something people have sort of overlooked or forgotten.

I'm not sure what happened to Ricky, why he felt compelled to take his own life. I've talked to Harold Pressley and others about it. Harold was probably his best friend. I don't think anybody had a clue that Ricky was having the kind of problems that drive someone to do that. Who knows what's going through someone's mind when they're thinking about suicide? We'll never know why.

I think we all get that way once in a while, where we don't see any way out of whatever problems we have, and we think, "Well maybe. ..." But things almost always seem to have a way of working out. Usually, problems go away, at least to some level, over time. There's no need to do something as drastic as Ricky did.

It was a tough time for me. I knew from a selfish standpoint— aside from losing a talented young man whom I had come to like— that, for all practical purposes, there was no chance for success with this franchise when that happened. Ricky was going to be a star, and we didn't have any. There was no Plan B. If Ricky had developed as everyone expected, there was a light at the end of the tunnel. Now that tunnel was dark for miles.

The team had a news conference to discuss the situation, and they asked me to speak. I got up in front of the media, and I just couldn't bring myself to say anything. That occasion was probably the only time in my life I've been speechless. I kept wondering, "Was there anything I could have done to prevent Ricky from doing this? Was there some kind of sign I should have seen?"

I'm sure everyone connected with the franchise was asking themselves the same questions and thinking, "I wish I could have talked to him that day. Maybe I could have said something to make him change his mind."

Ricky didn't get much playing time early in his rookie year. I didn't think he was quite ready, and I was old school in the sense that I liked to make rookies jump through a few hoops to appreciate their playing time. Some players believe that they're owed playing time just because they put on a jersey. And we had several guys at shooting guard and small forward who were probably better early on. But it had gotten to the point where Ricky started outplaying Derek Smith and Harold Pressley every day in practice, and all indications were that he was going to put in the effort to make himself an exceptional player. I had seen Ricky a week before at the summer league. He had worked hard on his body and was filling out. He looked ready to bust loose.

We had scored about 115 points per game the last 21 games of the 1988-89 season, going 11-10, and Ricky was a huge part of that. We were solid in the starting lineup at every spot other than center, so if we could get a big guy who could guard the basket with some skill, we would have a chance to excel. Unfortunately, we picked a bad year to win the draft lottery. We drafted Louisville's Pervis Ellison with the first pick. He was a lanky six-foot-10 shot-blocker who was nicknamed "Never Nervous Pervis" when he came into the league. Unfortunately, he didn't turn out to be a franchise kind of player; and it didn't take long for his nickname to become "Out of Service Pervis" because he was injured so often.

We needed help with that number-one pick, but there simply wasn't much available in that draft. The second pick that year was Danny Ferry, who had a rather limited career. Sean Elliott and Glen Rice went third and fourth, and they had nice careers but weren't franchise players. Stacey King was the fifth pick—he was the guy most of our fans seemed to want—and he probably wasn't as good as Pervis, as it turned out. He was a left-handed power forward from Oklahoma—much like Wayman Tisdale, except he was nowhere as good as Wayman. If you look back and evaluate it, the 14th pick, Tim Hardaway, was probably the best pick in that draft. Hindsight's always 20/20, and we should have taken Hardaway with our pick. But people would have thought we were crazy had we done that at the time, and had we done that, I don't know that he'd have made us significantly better, either.

Pervis did have some unique talents. Had his body held up, he might have been an impact player. He had one year—his third season, when he was with Washington—where he averaged 20 points and more than 10 rebounds. It was the kind of year that Bill Russell thought he'd have on a consistent basis. Of course, Pervis always had health issues. When you looked at Pervis, you could just see that his body wasn't going to hold up. Beyond that, he was a likable guy. But you got the impression that he didn't live for the opportunity to play basketball. He wasn't driven to be a great player. The game came easy to him—he had tremendous success at the college level, and, like many young people, the money he received as the first pick probably wounded his drive a bit.

Pervis came to camp injured. I think he hurt his foot during the summer, so he was out until well after the start of the season. We kept saying, "He'll be ready by camp," and camp came and went, then it was, "He'll be ready for the start of the season," and that came and went. At the end of the day, Pervis just wasn't a factor that year—or any year—for us.

Pervis's health was one of the reasons that, right before camp, we traded Jim Petersen for Ralph Sampson. Jim was undergoing knee surgery at the time of the trade. The Warriors waived his physical to make the deal happen, so you know how badly they wanted it to go through. Maybe that should have been a red flag, but the fact remains: at least Ralph could walk at the time, while Jim couldn't. We found out later that while Ralph could walk, he couldn't run. That's a bit of a problem in pro basketball.

Jim never played much for Golden State, and Ralph didn't play to any level for us, really. Everyone assumed the Kings got the worst end of the trade, but I'm not sure that's true. The salaries were almost the same; Russ had signed Jim to a big contract the year before, which is why the trade could be made. But Ralph Sampson was the big name and—as far as our fans were concerned—the big disappointment.

I never will forget the day that Ralph came to Sacramento. Bill and I met with him in Russ's office, just to sit down and talk for a while.

"Ralph," Russ said, "Stand up and let's see how high your reach is."

Ralph was seven foot two—everyone always said in college he was seven foot four, but he was a legit seven foot two—and Russ was maybe six foot 10. They stood flat-footed and reached, and Russ could reach about six inches over the top of Ralph's hand.

It flabbergasted me. I kind of came to understand that day—not that I didn't have an idea before—why Russ was one of the greatest players of all times. One of the reasons was that while Russ was six foot 10, he was really seven foot two because of that huge wingspan. Ralph was seven foot two with normal length for someone that tall, and Russ could reach right over the top of him.

Ralph's last real productive year had been in Houston. His first major knee injury happened the year after the Rockets went to the finals against Boston. He was traded to Golden State and got hurt again there. He was never the same player. Fans forget how good he'd been because of how his career ended. Maybe Ralph was never one of the five best players in the world, but he certainly had a couple of years, before major surgery, when he was one of the top 10 or 15. He was tall and very skilled, more comfortable facing the basket than being in the post, and he could run pretty well. His mobility had been one of the things that made him an exceptional big man. He and Hakeem Olajuwon were terrific together.

I always admired Ralph because he worked hard. When he was with us, Ralph couldn't play, and he caught all kinds of flak, but it wasn't because of effort. Behind the scenes, he really hit the weights and did everything he could to get healthy, but the knees were gone. You can't play NBA basketball without legs, and he didn't have any. In his two seasons with us, Ralph averaged 3.6 points and 3.8 rebounds. In the three seasons before he got hurt, he was a consistent 20 and 10 guy.

Most saw Ralph as a bitter, aloof player during his time in Sacramento. You probably see that to some degree with every star

Ralph Sampson tries to post up. *Jonathan Daniel/NBAE/Getty Images*

player who's trying to come back from a major injury, whether it's Penny Hardaway or Allan Houston or Chris Webber. Once the injuries begin, it's hard for a star player to realize that they're not quite the same. Having been a franchise kind of guy, it must have been difficult for Ralph to try to fit in as a marginal player (if even that).

Overall, I found Ralph easy to be around, very intelligent. He had trouble with the media because he always was asked the same question: Why aren't you Ralph Sampson anymore? It was sad to see players of minimal ability push him around on the floor. You could see him trying to get position, working his rear end off, and it was almost as if he was on skates. Other big guys could just bump him off the block.

We ended up waiving him before the start of the 1991-92 season. Team owner Gregg Lukenbill and I got together with Ralph and worked out a buyout. It wasn't a huge amount by NBA standards—it wouldn't even be an average NBA salary today, probably. Ralph really was very amenable. He still thought he could play, so he wanted to be waived and become a free agent. Of course, he couldn't. Washington picked him up and waived him. Then Ralph went overseas and was waived. It was a sorry ending, no doubt, and certainly not his fault. Injuries happen. They just seemed to happen to us more often than other teams.

The suicide was a huge blow. Neither Pervis nor Ralph was available early in the season. Wayman held out and arrived late to camp. Vinny Del Negro was hurt in camp. It was the worst of times. We had camp in Hawaii that year. Hawaii is paradise, right? I probably had the worst time in Hawaii that any tourist has ever had. I may not be the sharpest knife in the drawer, but I realized quickly that we didn't have any chance whatsoever to succeed. Forget about the injuries, holdouts, and lack of talent, all that—Ricky's suicide had enough impact by itself to ensure we'd have a long season.

Just how long was made clear in our first exhibition game. We played the Lakers—Magic Johnson, James Worthy, Kareem Abdul-Jabbar, and the rest—in Honolulu. The Lakers lined up Kareem for the center tap and we trotted out ... Randy Allen. Randy was an undrafted guy out of Florida State, maybe six foot eight. When he lined up against Kareem, it looked like a father-son game. The Lakers beat us handily in two games in Hawaii, as they should have. I don't think Kenny Smith played either game because of injuries; Danny Ainge maybe played one. I was pulling guys off the beach.

As a coach, what can you do?

I probably yelled, "Randy, damn it, why can't you guard Jabbar? What's wrong with you? Block that skyhook!"

Early in the regular season, Randy started against Rik Smits of the Pacers. I looked out on the floor, and Rik was wide open under the basket. I yelled, "Who's guarding Smits?"

All of the sudden I saw two little arms sticking out behind Rik. It was Randy. You literally couldn't see him—he was totally eclipsed—and that was our center. It looked like Rik had four arms: two high, regular ones, and two little ones underneath, like some Hindu god. I was like, "Holy cow!" Randy tried, bless his heart, but as they say, you can't teach height.

A week before Christmas, it was time for yet another shakeup. Ownership decided to get rid of Bill Russell. The Ralph trade was probably the capper; but looking back, Jim Petersen wouldn't have been doing anything for us either. I don't think Pervis had even played to that point. The team obviously didn't have much talent, and it was struggling.

I don't know how you could blame Russ for the Ricky Berry situation—Ricky had been a great pick in the first place. I'm sure the Kings would have liked to have fired me, too, but Russ had given me that nice contract extension.

Gregg Lukenbill called me in and told me what was going on and said, "You have a choice: You can continue to coach or move into the front office, whichever you want to do. You can take a couple of days to decide."

I really appreciated that. He was nicer to me than he had to be. I talked it over with my wife, Dodie.

"I'm going to be fired as a coach because this team can't win much," I told her. "Plus I'm miserable. The situation is just killing me, and it's probably changing my personality, making me a miserable little jerk to be around."

She and my kids—Jay and Danielle—certainly agreed with that. It became an easy choice for me to make, a chance to stay employed and move upstairs and be involved in hiring the next coach. At least that's what I thought at the time.

I coached the team for another couple of weeks while we searched for my replacement. My feeling was that I would never coach again. Although there were players and times I really enjoyed, it just wasn't as satisfying an experience as I'd imagined. I was at the pinnacle of my profession and feeling no sense of pride about it. Because of the circumstances I was put in, I just didn't see any chance to be competitive. I felt like the Kings were the little neighborhood grocery store competing against the Safeway across the street. I did the best I could. I'm sure there are coaches who could have won more games, but I'm not sure they would have won too many more games. Pat Riley's a better coach than I am, no doubt. But I also know that if his first job had been with the Kings with the exact same personnel that I had, and my first job had been coaching Worthy, Magic, and Kareem, there's no doubt things would have gone better for me and worse for Pat.

I was sad when they let Russ go. As I said, I really liked him. He was always good to me. He felt the team owed me something, that I had been taken advantage of a little, so he gave me the contract extension that helped keep me employed. He looked after my interest, and I knew that. Russ handled being fired pretty well. He could see it wasn't going to work, and he had a long-term contract, so he could get on with his life. He didn't like Sacramento that much—Seattle had become his home—so it wasn't as tough for him as it could have been. He took more than his share of hits around the country, but when it was all over, he was still considered the greatest winner of all time.

The search for a new coach was one of the most disappointing things I've been involved in during my time with the Kings. Rick Benner—who was then the club president—owners Joe Benvenuti and Gregg Lukenbill, and I were the search committee. We brought in several good candidates—including John MacLeod, Bobby Weiss, and Mike Schuler—for interviews. Dick Motta was a latecomer. Now, he was a big-time winner with a well-deserved reputation, but we didn't handle the situation well. Motta didn't have to go through the same process the other candidates had. He got right to the owners and kind of let them know that he was interested in the job, but he didn't feel as though he needed to go through the same level of scrutiny as the others. I understand he was looking for an edge, but he was hired under different criteria than the other candidates had faced.

Dick came on board and created a little stir for a short time. But the truth of the matter is, the team simply wasn't very good, and a new coach wasn't going to make much difference. We were 9-19 when Dick took over and, percentage-wise, all we did was tread water the rest of the season. At the end of the day, players are players, and we didn't have enough. Honestly, I thought Dick would have a little more impact than he did.

Dick came in, unlike Russ, and said, "I'm a plodder."

He didn't promise the championships or even the playoffs right away, so at least he was honest. It was kind of an early view into Dick. When he was interviewing for the job, he was very optimistic, which is what we wanted. The owners were getting restless. The fans were getting restless.

"We can do this," Dick said. "We can play considerably better with some minor adjustments, blah, blah, blah."

Then, once he got the job, his outlook immediately changed. Before we hired him, Dick told us how much he liked our roster. He thought he could coach Ralph and Rodney and Danny, but within about a month, he didn't like any of them. He felt we needed to shake things up and go with a younger squad. He wanted the chance to mold young guys. Eventually, that's the direction we went, and that didn't work, either.

The veterans tuned Dick out quickly. Once, Dick was trying to make a point to the team. He waved his championship ring around and said, "This is why you should listen to me."

Danny Ainge—he wasn't trying to start a mutiny, just being a smartass—said, "Coach, I have two of those. Maybe they should listen to *me*."

Dick just hated that.

During the interview process, John MacLeod seemed to be the candidate who was the most optimistic about our chances—not that he could have done any better, but it would probably have been an easier sell with the fans, and his honeymoon period would have lasted longer than Dick's. Over the years, Dick might have been the worst fit for the time he was here of all the coaches we had. He'd been a great coach and won a championship with Washington, but the league had changed, the players had changed, and Dick didn't. What made him a terrific coach in Chicago in the '70s didn't really work in the '90s—that and the fact that we didn't have Jerry Sloan, Bob Love, and Norm Van Lier on our roster.

I always thought that Dick Motta, Cotton Fitzsimmons, Bill Fitch, and John MacLeod—when they came into the NBA in the late '60s and early '70s—had an impact on the league. They were good college coaches who changed what coaching was at the pro level. Yet, while someone like Cotton evolved, Dick stayed the same. As the players changed, he didn't change how he dealt with them or his style of play, whereas Cotton made adjustments and succeeded with different kinds of players and teams. Dick had his way, and with the right kind of players, it would work without question. Unfortunately, we didn't have that kind of players, and it was going to be very hard to get them. We never could.

We did try, though. About a month after Motta took over, we traded Kenny Smith to Atlanta and brought in Antoine Carr, which gave us what came to be known as the "beef and pork" lineup with Carr and Tisdale. One thing about Dick: He coached great halfcourt offense, one geared for particularly burly forwards who could score on the block. If you were a forward and couldn't put up big numbers with Dick, you weren't very good. Conversely, some of the guards didn't take to the system very well.

Kenny was one of them, but the trade was a good one for us because Kenny wasn't the star we thought he might be. Atlanta traded for him and later waived him. Kenny finally found himself as a reserve with Houston. He's become more of a star after the fact. Fortunately, after he was waived, he figured things out and found a way to become a valuable role player.

People may wonder how Kenny—certainly not a big-name guy like Charles Barkley—came to be such a well-known TV commentator. Kenny owes that to Michael Jackson, who played with us for a couple of seasons in that era. Jackson was a very bright, tough kid who played on a championship team at Georgetown as well as on the team Villanova beat for the 1985 championship. He became an executive with Turner Sports and hired Kenny. Kenny's personality and talent have come out since then, but if Michael hadn't had hired him, I don't know that Kenny would have been on anybody's radar screen as a TV color guy. It certainly has turned out well for him.

However, that season didn't turn out well for us. We finished 23-59—low tide for the franchise. Dick wanted to clean house and get a fresh start. We ended up getting a transfusion of new blood, all right, but what we really needed was a heart transplant.

CHAPTER TEN

Welcome to Hell

During the Dick Motta era, for the first time, players wanted to be traded from Sacramento and didn't want to be traded to the Kings. There's a misconception about the Kings—that because Sacramento is a small market that doesn't have the kind of nightlife you find in Los Angeles or New York, players didn't want to come here. But in the earliest years of the franchise, players didn't seem to object too strenuously to being on the Kings. But Dick quickly became unhappy with all the players; the players didn't like his system; and the situation became uglier.

We traded Pervis Ellison in a three-way deal with Washington and Utah just before the 1990 draft. We decided to cut our losses, and Dick liked the idea of getting guard Bobby Hansen, who had been on some good teams in Utah, and young center Eric Leckner, plus a first-round draft pick. You had to be aware of anyone the Jazz traded in those years: John Stockton and Karl Malone made everyone on that team look a little better than they actually were. Hansen was a limited role player, and we needed a little more than that. He finished up with the Bulls and had a couple of moments in the sun, but neither he nor Leckner helped us much. Later on, Pervis had one good year with Washington, but it probably ended up hurting the

Bullets because they ended up giving him a big, new contract, which they came to regret.

A day after that big trade, we sent Rodney McCray to Dallas for Bill Wennington and two more first-rounders, so we ended up with four first-round draft choices. We were the first team ever to have that many—and the last. Teams saw how we fared and said, "We don't want to do that."

Later that summer, we traded Danny Ainge to Portland for, essentially, a bag of rocks.

Lionel Simmons was the seventh pick in the draft, and he ended up second in the Rookie of the Year vote behind Derrick Coleman. Travis Mays was the 14th pick and played fairly well as a rookie but never developed. We took Duane Causwell, a seven-foot center, at 18. Generally, people saw him as a bit of a disappointment, but he had a 10-year career and set a couple of franchise blocked-shot records, so you can't say he was a mistake. We took Anthony Bonner at number 23, and he had a decent career in the NBA as an undersized and often out-of-control power forward.

Anybody who knows the NBA understands that, unless you get a franchise guy, it's very difficult to change your team through the draft. We certainly didn't. All we accomplished was changing from a veteran team that didn't work out to a young team that didn't work at all.

For the first time since college, I wasn't sitting on the bench as part of a coaching staff. As time passed, I missed coaching to some degree during the wins, but I didn't miss it all during the losses. For the most part, I didn't miss it at all.

My job as player personnel director, as I saw it, was to get a roster that Dick liked. He came in with a certain amount of authority, which he deserved, given that he was the third-winningest coach in NBA history. Even though I was inexperienced in the front office, I felt like I knew the league and the talent. I came to realize that Dick, more than most coaches, got down on guys pretty quickly and sometimes wanted change for the sake of change. I know now—from being around Geoff Petrie for a number of years—that change for change's sake is not a good way to go.

Patience is a virtue. Had I been in a stronger position back then, maybe known a little more about it and been more confident, we might not have made some of the deals we made. However, at the time, I wanted to help Dick make whatever moves he wanted, because I figured he knew what he was doing. The truth of the matter is, he didn't know what to do, personnel-wise. He was a coach, and as a coach, he too often became caught up in the ebb and flow of what had happened in the last game.

We lost 13 of 14 games to start the season, and the only win was our one and only road victory of the season, at Washington. With all the young guys, I figured we'd take our lumps, but that was too lumpy. We had some decent young talent; still, we weren't as talented as we had been the previous season. We had traded veteran guys who maybe weren't quite good enough to lead teams but were good enough to be part of good teams. We ended up with a large group of guys with a great deal to prove. We proved that you can't play four rookies significant minutes and win—unless you have Amare Stoudemire and Dwayne Wade on the same team, and we certainly didn't.

Of the four rookies, Lionel was the only guy you could count as being a legitimate, top-flight NBA player. "Train," as we called Lionel, was a guy who really benefited from Dick's system. We weren't a running team, and Train certainly wasn't known for his leg speed. Yet he was a darned good player—probably as good a rebounding small forward as there was in the league. He could defend big guards, small forwards, and some power forwards. He was by far more tough-minded and skilled than he was athletic. He could score on the block. Because he wasn't a great jumper or very quick, he probably had more shots blocked than anyone in America. Still, I remember one game he had around 43 points and 18 rebounds against Charles Barkley in Philly, so he was a capable guy.

Train should have had a better career than he did. He had just enough leg speed and jumping ability to get things done, and when he lost some of that due to knee problems, he became a marginal player. He couldn't rebound well enough, and he couldn't post up, which was more important, because Train never had that outside game. He might have been an all-star caliber player had he stayed healthy.

Olden Polynice and Lionel "Train" Simmons rest during a free throw.
Rocky Widner/NBAE/Getty Images

The low point of the season—one of the low points in the team's history—was a 101-59 loss in Charlotte. I didn't see it, but I listened to it on the radio while I was out for a walk. Our radio announcer, Gary Gerould, is brilliant at painting a picture with words, so I could see how ugly it really was. On the trip home that night, Dick said he was going to resign, that he'd had enough, and Wayman Tisdale and some of the other guys talked him out of it.

Later on, Wayman told me, "Boy, I wish we hadn't done that."

Charlotte wasn't a real good team at that time, and our 59 points was the lowest by a team since 1955. I'm sure it stung Dick, because he prided himself on his halfcourt offense. What's ironic is that the veteran guys we'd gotten rid of—Rodney McCray and Danny Ainge—even if they didn't run the offense exactly the way Dick wanted to, they could make it work. Our young guys weren't as adept at running it.

In fairness to Dick, as the year went along, the team got better at it. We became a good homecourt team. I always said that season was one where the crowd helped us win some games. We'd be a terror at home, and then go on the road and just lay eggs. With Wayman Tisdale, Antoine Carr, and Lionel Simmons, we had three guys who could put up good numbers. Many teams couldn't match up with them. But we lost 37 straight road games that year, which was simply amazing to me. The law of averages says you're going to win a couple by accident over that span.

I went to Dick at one point and said, "Whatever we're doing in terms of preparation or how we're approaching road games, we need to change. If you find yourself in a hole, the first thing you do is stop digging."

The trouble was, neither Dick nor I had an answer for it. We were very competitive at home, and not only did we lose on the road, we were blown out frequently. There shouldn't be that kind of discrepancy. The mark of an excellent team is to go 21-20 on the road, a winning record. That is not a great percentage, but at the end of every year, there will be five or six teams in the league with winning road records, and almost invariably the NBA champion will be one of those teams. The Suns were remarkable last season with 31 wins on the road.

We finished the 1990-91 season with 25 wins and headed into a busy off-season. We took Syracuse forward Billy Owens with the number-three pick in the draft, then got forward/center Pete Chilcutt from North Carolina later in the first round and New Mexico State guard Randy Brown in the second.

Shortly after the draft, we were able to send Travis Mays to Atlanta for Spud Webb, which I think was one of the best trades that I ever made. We needed a point guard badly, and we knew Travis wasn't going to be able to make the adjustment. I learned a valuable lesson from Travis: You can't assume that players can change positions. Certainly, special ones can: Jerry West played forward at West Virginia, and Oscar Robertson played forward at Cincinnati, and they both turned out to be decent guards. But it's not automatic, and the reality is that many can't make the adjustment, especially to point guard, which is the hardest position to play.

Spud was truly a marvel at five foot seven, so tough and durable for his size. He was a really good guy, but it took a while to get to know him. Dodie and I picked him up at the airport after the trade to take him to our training camp at the University of California-Davis. Much like Rodney McCray, Spud didn't want to be traded because he was going from a very good team to a bad one. He was not a happy camper. I don't think he said two words during the half-hour car ride.

Afterwards, Dodie said, "Wow ... he's really an unfriendly guy."

"Well," I said. "He is now."

Bobby Hansen, who was traded to Chicago two games into the season, welcomed Spud to camp by saying, "Welcome to hell."

Spud was one of the truly great athletes to play in the NBA. He was almost Jordan-like in that sense. Everyone knows that Spud won the slam-dunk championship, and that was special. More importantly, Spud could change the game. I remember scouting in Boston during Spud's rookie year. The Hawks put Spud in, and there was Dennis Johnson, one of the all-time great defenders, giving him 10-12 feet of room so Spud wouldn't just blow by him. And Spud would still zip-zap right to the free-throw line and get a little jumper. I said to myself, "Self, this is something to remember." With us, Spud also turned himself into a great free throw shooter and three-point shooter. That helped him at his size, as he got older and lost a bit of his quickness.

There were still a couple of significant moves to come before the season began. We traded Antoine Carr to San Antonio for seven-foot-two center Dwayne Schintzius and a second-round draft pick.

I remember Antoine came to me once and said, "I'm only making $900,000; and I can't live on that."

Now, at the time, $900,000 wasn't too shabby, even by NBA standards. "Antoine, I don't know much," I said. "But I know that if you can't live on $900,000, you probably can't live on $2 million or $4 million."

Of course, Antoine had a point: Wayman was making tons more money than he was, and Antoine felt he was as good a player. Whether Antoine or Wayman was better, I can't say. It was close, and their salaries weren't.

Spud Webb blows by defenders. *Andy Hayt/NBAE/Getty Images*

Dick felt he wanted a big center, a Tom Boerwinkle-type who could pass and work in his high-post offense. He liked what he saw in Schintzius, and that proved to be a terrible mistake. Dwayne had some of those talents, and the guy could have been a good player, no doubt about it. I'm not sure he liked to play, to compete, or work. You saw the same thing when he played with other teams. He was a frustrating guy.

Speaking of frustrating, we also decided to cut ties with Ralph Sampson. There were two years left on his contract when we bought him out. He was happy to go, thinking that things would change for the better if he was somewhere else. We were happy to turn the page.

Prior to the draft, I had talked to Don Nelson of the Warriors about the possibility of trading the third overall pick for Mitch Richmond. He said he had no interest in doing that. I thought it was worth throwing out there because, while they were a good team, they were locked into playing small ball. They had that great "Run T-M-C" combination—Tim Hardaway, Mitch, and Chris Mullin.

I thought they might want to use the pick to get Dikembe Mutombo, because they needed a center, and even though he couldn't score, it didn't matter, because they had scorers. They needed defense and rebounding. We needed everything, but more than anything else, we needed a star, regardless of position. I thought Mitch Richmond—former rookie of the year, proven 22-points-per-game scorer—was a no-risk guy for us.

After the draft, Nellie came back to me about Owens. We hadn't signed him yet, and his agent swore that he'd never sign with us, but people made more of that than they should have. That had nothing to do with the trade; we would have traded Billy for Mitch if Billy was signed, sealed, delivered, and went around saying, "My goal in life has always been to be a King."

"Well, we want Billy Owens," Nellie said. "But we don't want to give up Mitch."

He had two or three different offers, but I told him, "We'll trade Billy for Mitch, and that's it. If not, we'll get him signed and he'll play for us."

As time went on, we reached an agreement with Billy on a contract, and Nellie came back and said, "Let's do it."

All the brilliant Bay Area sports writers reported that the Kings had been taken advantage of, and it certainly proved out that wasn't the case. Billy rebounded well for a small forward, but he wasn't the big guy who was going to solve the problems they had, and he didn't shoot well enough to be a star. He was sort of like Rodney McCray in that respect.

Mitch came here and was very unhappy. It was a very tough time for us after the trade. We wanted Mitch, but he didn't want to be here. He didn't like Dick's offense. The biggest part was that he wanted to be at Golden State. Once a little time passed, Mitch and Spud ended up being very good together. We made some real strides there with those two trades.

Mitch was our first real all-star player, although you could make the argument that both Reggie Theus and Danny Ainge were worthy in their time with us. In my mind, Mitch was a guy we could start to build a franchise around. Now, he wasn't a guy necessarily good enough to lead you—he wasn't Magic or Bird or Jordan or Duncan—but I've always said, if Mitch was your second best player, you're probably a 50-win team. Unfortunately, for all the years he was here, he was our first-best. We just never could get that better player to go with him.

Mitch never fully bought into Dick's system. Dick did give him plenty of freedom—or maybe Mitch just decided to do what he wanted to do. The problem was that not only were we a bad team, but we were boring to watch much of the time, very predictable. Early during the '91-92 season, Boston came to town, and Larry Bird came to my house for dinner.

"Motta's been running the same stuff for years," he told me. "I know your offense as well as your players do."

There was one play in particular—I think Dick called it a "get"—that we ran all the time. "I know where you sit in the stands," Larry said to me. "When they run that play, I'm going to step right in front of the low-post guy and steal the ball, then I'm going to turn and look at you."

Sure enough, the first time we ran that play, Bird stole the ball, turned to look at me sitting behind the basket, and smiled. Larry was a pretty smart player.

Mitch "The Rock" Richmond drives baseline. *Rocky Widner/NBAE/Getty Images*

Dick also had a practice drill where he'd put a folding chair at the foul line and have the players shoot over it. It was something he brought to college from junior high school and to the NBA from college—not that it hurt anything, but I don't think anyone thought it made you a better player. After one shootaround on the road, Pete Chilcutt was really in a giddy mood.

"I did it!" He yelled. "I did it! I knew I could do it!"

"Pete, what the hell are you talking about?" I asked.

"I've scored on a chair in every arena in the league now!" he said.

In late November, we ended our record 43-game road losing streak by beating Orlando 95-93. It was wearing on everybody, and I couldn't understand how we could be so competitive at home—and look impressive at times—but not beat anybody on the road. Chilcutt made some big free throws down the stretch, and Wayman Tisdale won a jump ball and batted the ball downcourt to let the time run out—kind of a Vlade Divac-type move that actually worked. Fortunately, there wasn't an evil power forward out there ready to shoot a three-pointer and win the game.

Dick Motta was fired on Christmas Eve with a 7-18 record. He had gone 48-113 (a .298 winning percentage) with the club. The timing was unfortunate, but he had forced the team's hand. Dick had a tendency to sour on veteran players very quickly, and he already was griping about Mitch a little.

Gregg Lukenbill, the team owner, told me, "I don't believe Dick likes anybody, and if doesn't like Mitch, we have no answers."

Then, during his pregame radio show in San Antonio on December 23, Dick laid out his plan to retire at the end of the season. He hadn't consulted anyone in the front office before doing that. I didn't hear it, but Rick Benner, the team president, called me because Gregg had heard it and was very offended. Gregg thought that Dick basically was dictating what was going to happen; and his feeling was, if Dick was planning to leave anyhow, better sooner than later. Really, I don't think Dick was too unhappy about it. Coaching the Kings wasn't doing his legacy much good.

We decided to move up the top assistant coach, Rex Hughes. He was in a situation similar to what I'd experienced before Bill Russell was hired. He made the team better; he opened up the offense, and the players seemed to try harder than they had under Dick. Rex really wanted the job, maybe to a fault. The second game he coached was against the Bulls in Chicago. The Bulls were a good team—not great at that time—and they beat us. We were at the old Chicago Stadium, which was in a bad part of town. Rex was angry and frustrated because he didn't think the team had given a good effort, so he decided to walk back to the hotel rather than take the team bus—about five miles through gang territory.

As mad as Rex was—and he was a big guy—the gang-bangers probably said, "We'll leave this guy alone. If he's crazy enough to walk through this area, we don't want to mess with him."

I thought Rex probably showed enough the rest of the season, going 22-35, to get a shot at coaching the next season. Rex really set his heart on getting that job. Unfortunately, his timing was bad.

Gregg Lukenbill had decided to sell the team.

CHAPTER ELEVEN

Down in the Ditch

There's an old joke that goes like this:

"How do you make a small fortune in the restaurant business?"

"Start with a large fortune."

That quip probably applies to Gregg Lukenbill, the managing partner of the Kings. Luke had made a small fortune as a developer. I don't know if he ever saw the Kings as the way to make a larger pile, but that certainly didn't happen—any profit he made probably was plowed back into the mortgage on Arco Arena. When he bought into the NBA, you didn't need to have hundreds of millions of dollars to be an owner, although that never hurt. After nine seasons as the front man of the ownership group, Luke was going through hard financial times, and he could no longer keep up with the other basketball Joneses.

Luke asked me if I knew anyone around the league who could put him in touch with potential buyers. I called Jerry West, who knew Jim Thomas—a Los Angeles developer who had some well-heeled partners who were interested in purchasing a team. One of his partners was Eli Broad, one of the nation's biggest homebuilders. The Thomas group bought 53 percent of the Kings and Arco Arena for $140 million in April of 1992. Jerry West got a finder's fee, and I got a handshake and a pat on the back—not that I expected anything more. Jerry had played golf with Jim Thomas in L.A. and arranged to put Jim in touch with Luke.

Jim and his partners bought the Kings and kept me around because I knew the personnel. Jim wanted me to contact candidates for our head-coaching job. Our head scout, Scotty Stirling, Jim, team president Rick Benner and I were the search committee. We interviewed Rex Hughes, who did a great job in his short time as head coach and certainly deserved to be a candidate. But it quickly became obvious that Jim's group wanted a fresh start, and Rex was out of the picture.

Overall, the ownership change was considered positive. Jim's group had more wherewithal than Luke did; and Jim had a good basketball background. The unfortunate thing was that, by the time he sold the team, Gregg Lukenbill had become a terrific owner. He understood what he didn't know about the game and had come to grips with the need to listen to his basketball people and let them make the basketball decisions.

Being an owner is just like being a coach or player—experience helps. Jim came in slightly better prepared than Gregg had been, but he still had never been part of a professional sports team. In my experience, most businessmen who've never been around pro sports think they can run their team as they do their businesses. It doesn't work that way, because sports teams, unlike businesses, have fans who get emotional and demanding. Most people know more about the teams they cheer for than the companies their 401k money is invested in, which, when you think about it, is pretty strange. By the time Jim sold the team, he had become a terrific owner, too, but we had a number of disagreements along the way.

Our candidates for the coaching job aside from Rex were solid guys: John Wetzel, Randy Pfund, Del Harris, Mike Fratello, and Garry St. Jean. I contacted Chuck Daly and Doug Moe, and both of them essentially said, "I'm interested if your ownership group wants to fly out to see me, and it's going to cost you a bunch of money." Fratello and Del had proven winning records. Randy was an assistant coach with Pat Riley for a number of years. Saint had been with

Don Nelson. Wetzel had been with Rick Adelman and Jack Ramsay, and he had been an interim head coach with the Suns.

Wetzel's interview stood out, but not because of his coaching philosophy: We interviewed him in Santa Monica during the Rodney King riots in Los Angeles. The area we were in didn't have any problems, but we had to give John a ride back to the Forum, which was too close for comfort to the action. It was a scary time. You could see smoke from fires everywhere, and all you could hear were sirens. We ended up driving back to Sacramento because it was nearly impossible to get a flight out.

I thought Fratello and Harris were the best-prepared candidates if we weren't going to keep Rex, and Scotty Stirling and Rick Benner seemed to feel the same way. However, Jim Thomas thought Garry St. Jean was more optimistic and positive. Saint seemed to believe that our team's talent was better than the record indicated. Mike and Del were a little more knowledgeable in their assessment of our roster. Naturally, Jim wanted to hear that his new team could win 50 games. That came with being a new owner.

We had some decent talent—Spud and Mitch at guard, Train and Tisdale at forward—and we drafted swingman Walt "The Wizard" Williams out of Maryland with the seventh pick. He was named to the all-rookie first team. But we had no depth and very little in the middle. Duane Causwell—who could block shots but little else—was our center.

We introduced Saint as the head coach on May 22, and it was announced that I had a new title, too: I had been the director of player personnel, and suddenly, I was the general manager. I was kind of an afterthought. Honestly, it dawned on Jim that he probably should have someone with that title in place when Saint was hired, so I got a promotion. While it was nice to get the opportunity, I knew there were going to be problems. As much as I liked Garry St. Jean, he wasn't the so-called committee's choice—he was Jim's choice. I was hired as GM without a contract, which wasn't a real confidence-builder, so I knew I wasn't Jim's guy. Honestly, *he* was the general manager.

Over the years, I interviewed in a number of places for different jobs: Houston, Minnesota, Portland, maybe some others. I don't think any of the jobs involved working in the ticket booth or the

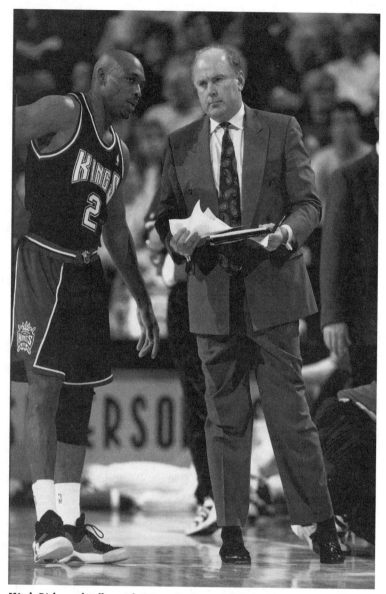

Mitch Richmond talks with Garry St. Jean. *Jeff Reinking/NBAE/Getty Images*

concession stand. Jim and I got along well, and we liked each other, and I didn't want to leave the Kings. However, I knew that being the GM probably was a temporary situation, and I just needed to try to make the best of it.

The 1992-93 season was another of those ho-hum 25-win affairs, although there were some very positive signs. We ended a 43-game losing streak that went back to 1974 on the Lakers' home court. That was a huge win for Jim and the rest of the owners because they all lived in Los Angeles and knew all the big shots at Lakers games. "The Wizard" had a big game, which earned me brownie points with Jim because I had pushed to draft Walt.

We beat Dallas 139-81—the most lopsided win in franchise history—right after Christmas. We followed that up with a 56-point win over Philadelphia—the largest margins of victory in consecutive games in NBA history. Mitch became our first all-star since 1981. Unfortunately, he couldn't play because he broke his thumb. While we had moments when we looked like a powerhouse, in the end, injuries to Mitch and others just crushed us.

We improved to 28-54 the next season—the first time in five seasons that we didn't finish last in our division. Mitch became the first King since Otis Birdsong in 1980-81 named All-NBA; he was on the second team after finishing seventh in scoring at 23.4 points per game. He also was the first Kings player since Nate Archibald in 1975 to start in the All-Star Game.

But all anyone really remembers about that season was Bobby Hurley's accident.

We took Bobby with the seventh pick in 1993. That draft was a mixed bag: Chris Webber was the No. 1 pick, followed by Shawn Bradley, Anfernee Hardaway, Jamal Mashburn, J.R. Rider, Calbert Cheaney, Bobby, Vin Baker, Rodney Rogers, and Lindsey Hunter. I thought Bobby could be maybe a John Stockton-type player. He had a much better college career than Stockton did. Bobby was the all-time assist leader in the NCAA and had the best college three-point shooting percentage of anyone we ever drafted. He was a high school All-American, his high school team had won two national championships, and he was co-MVP of the McDonald's game, so the pedigree was there.

Bobby's up-court speed while dribbling the ball was almost the same as his sprint without it, which was remarkable. Bobby had played in some tune-up games against the Dream Team, and Charles Barkley and Larry Bird told me that Bobby and C-Webb were the two college players who really stood out. They had to put Michael Jordan on Bobby to keep him from penetrating all the time—Stockton couldn't stay in front of him.

"One thing that Bobby can do—he makes passes that lead to lay-ups," Stockton told me. "And not many guards in this league can do that."

Coming from one of the greatest passers of all time, I thought that was revealing.

So there were many people who thought Bobby would be pretty good, even though quite a few of our fans said we shouldn't have drafted him—after the accident, of course. Obviously, Bobby didn't turn out to be a star, but it's not like Vin Baker or Rodney Rogers turned out to be, either. At least Bobby had a legitimate excuse for not developing into a major player. The rest of them don't—other than talent.

Bobby showed what he might have become in some early flashes—a 14-assist game and a couple of 20-point games in the first 19 games of the season—and he had that special quickness. He was only averaging seven points and wasn't shooting well, but there was no reason to doubt that he was on the right track. People were impatient with him because they don't understand that point guards generally take time to develop. Gary Payton, John Stockton, Kevin Johnson … it took them all two or three years to find their games. It's a process. We also didn't play a style that fit him very well. Bobby didn't make mistakes in the open floor, but we never got in the open floor. We didn't play that way. I don't mean to dump on Mitch, but I think he hurt the running game. He didn't want to run, because he knew he was going to get to shoot anyway. Had Bobby come along at the same time Jason Williams did, he might not have been as flashy as Jason, but he might have been more effective in the running game.

Thinking about how good Bobby might been—what he might have meant to the franchise—is a moot point. We lost to the

A healthy Bobby Hurley attacks Karl Malone. *Andy Hayt/NBAE/Getty Images*

Clippers at Arco on December 12. I was at home when I got the call from Rick Benner: Bobby had been in a wreck. Someone ran a stop sign and smashed into him. He was found alive but unconscious and severely injured, his car in a ditch near the arena.

While the accident certainly was tragic, the other side of it was that Bobby was very lucky to be alive. Everything fell in place, or he would be dead. During that evening, the doctors felt he was going to die a couple of times. If Mike Peplowski, our rookie center, hadn't been right behind him on the road to help pull him out ... if there hadn't happened to be a specialist around who could reattach Bobby's trachea ... if Bobby hadn't been in tremendous physical shape—all those things fell into place. You'd better believe I flashed back a few times to the Ricky Berry episode and the auto accident I had had in my younger days.

There was some question about whether Bobby would be able to live a normal life, let alone play NBA basketball again. The remarkable thing is, he played 68 games for us the following season. Even more remarkable: Our fans didn't give him much of a honeymoon period before they got down on him. I thought that was one of the cruelest things I'd ever seen. I was very disappointed to see Kings fans act that way toward a player. The frustration with the team spilled over onto Bobby. He became an easy target. But the truth is, 99 percent of players—had they been in an accident like that—would never have played again.

Jay Williams from Duke—Chicago's No. 2 pick in 2002—was in a motorcycle accident a few seasons ago and hasn't played since. His injuries weren't as severe as Bobby's, and Bobby was back trying to play in the summer league within six months. Looking back, it was foolish of us to allow that. But it shows you the courage and the dedication Bobby had. But he was a six-foot guard who had lost some of his quickness due to knee injuries, had lost a great left hand due to a torn-up shoulder, and seemed one hard foul away from going back to the hospital. Here was a kid who was trying, and by trying, he was getting weaker and weaker as the year continued. He couldn't keep on any weight. He should have been given more slack.

About two weeks after Bobby's accident, I resigned as general manager. The main reason was that Jim Thomas wanted to fire Garry St. Jean. Even though Saint wasn't my first choice, I didn't think that was really fair. He hadn't been given enough time, and with what happened to Bobby and the impact that had on the team's mental state, there was no way to judge Saint as a coach. I knew it wasn't going well for the team, or me, and Jim and I weren't communicating as well as we should. So I told him, "Maybe a change would help, and I'd be willing to step back."

I made up my mind when I had a chance to trade Lionel Simmons for Detlef Schrempf. I went to Jim for permission, and he said, "I don't know much about Detlef."

"Well, I do," I said. "And you have to trust me on this."

But he didn't, which was his right even though he was wrong. He didn't have confidence in me, and maybe he had good reason.

I agreed to stay on to help Jim select my replacement and ended up being the GM-without-title the rest of the season. The situation was unusual and uncomfortable. As he went through the process and talked to some candidates, I think I looked a little better to Jim. When it came time to make the hire, he could see that I knew the league, I knew the people involved, and I had some ideas about what needed to be done. Jim and I went through a rocky patch there. That happens in the best of marriages, right?

I even made a substantial trade in that period, sending Pete Chilcutt and future draft picks to Detroit for Olden Polynice. OP ended up being one of the most reviled players in Sacramento history because he popped off about the city and the fans once he was done with us. But when he first came to the Kings, he probably was the best center we'd had since LaSalle Thompson—maybe better than Tank—and he helped improve the team.

Olden's problems weren't as a player, although he wasn't an all-star by any means. He simply couldn't get along with people for any length of time. He was a little hard to deal with primarily because he had himself pegged as a better player than he was. I'd say his teammates got along with him, but it wasn't a 50-50 kind of thing. To get along with OP, you had to go 70-30. But whatever problems he had here, he had more problems in other places. Saint was able to get OP to play—Olden averaged nearly a double-double for five of his first six seasons with us—but it *had* to be a challenge.

Saint's mantra was "positive mental attitude," and his public face was inevitably upbeat. On a day-to-day basis, that's somewhat how he was. Now, after games he wasn't like that—like any coach. Saint had a dark side—after losses, he would get as bitter and cynical as anyone else—except maybe Dick Motta. To his credit, the next day he'd be over it. He'd bounce back pretty well. Saint was a competitive guy, and losing is losing. He'd get mad at players—probably everybody except Mitch, which was smart on his part. He figured out early that Mitch would determine what level of success we'd have. Definitely, on those plane rides after losses, there wasn't much positive mental attitude flowing out of Saint. Of course, OP could do that to a coach all by himself.

CHAPTER TWELVE

A Change at the Top

One of the best things I ever did with the Kings was to encourage Jim Thomas to hire Geoff Petrie, who had helped put together some powerhouse teams in Portland. Jim was in a hurry to make a decision after I resigned, but I told Jim that he'd be better off waiting, that there would be quality candidates available at the end of the season, because that's the way things work in the league. I had a good idea that Geoff might be on the market, and I thought that not only would Geoff be good here, but he'd be terrific working with Jim.

Geoff joined us in early June of 1994 and had an immediate impact. As Jim's guy, he was allowed more freedom than I had been, and he put it to good use, upgrading our scouting system and the time we put into it. Geoff brought a lot of class and organizational ability over and above his basketball knowledge, and that has continued to this day. He has improved the franchise dramatically.

Jim asked me to remain with the team in a different position, but when Geoff was hired, I told him he didn't have to honor that commitment. Looking back, it was probably pretty silly to do that. He might have said, "OK, get out of here." Instead, he wanted me to hang around, and I don't think I've had a bad day working with Geoff.

We had a terrific draft in '94. We picked power forward Brian Grant in the first round, and he ended up being a first-team all-rookie selection. We got two other beefy guys, Michael Smith and Lawrence Funderburke, in the second round. The draft remade our team. Mitch was a tough guy, and while Olden really wasn't, he became more of one with the new guys around, and we intimidated many teams.

Grant essentially replaced Wayman Tisdale, who left as a free agent. Wayman had a nice run with us. He had respectable numbers, was very popular, and was just a class guy. On the other hand, he's a good example of an old saying: Even bad teams have leading scorers. In other words, just because a guy scores a lot of points doesn't mean he can truly make a team better. With teams that aren't very good—like ours at that time—you can make a lot of trades that are some-what favorable, but it doesn't necessarily mean you're going to become significantly better. You trade a marginal guy for another marginal guy. And guess what: You're still kind of marginal. The NBA is a star league, and until you get a star or two, little can happen.

Did we miss Wayman's scoring? Well, we went 39-43, the most wins we'd had in a season since 1982-83. We missed the playoffs by one game. We lost our last game of the season—102-89 at Denver—in a play-or-go-home game. Mitch was his normal brilliant self, the MVP of the All-Star Game in Phoenix and a second-team All-NBA selection after averaging 22.8 points.

Until a certain power forward from Michigan came to us a few years later, Mitch Richmond was the closest thing we had to a super-star. But people need to know that as good as Mitch was for the Kings, we were very good for him, too, and in that regard, things may have been unequal. Mitch had name recognition on a national basis, which we hadn't had in several seasons. But, in my mind, this franchise did everything it could to allow Mitch to become a national name and an all-star. If he had stayed in Golden State, I'm not sure that would have happened for him because Tim Hardaway and Chris Mullin were there, and Mitch wasn't the focus of the offense.

In the years since he left Sacramento, Mitch has come to under-stand and appreciate that. Like many players, he didn't appreciate

Mitch Richmond raises his All-Star Game MVP trophy.
Andrew D. Bernstein/NBAE/Getty Images

the situation he was in at the time. One of the real problems I had with Mitch is that he was a high-maintenance guy. I felt like, "Why can't we do enough for you? What are we supposed to do?" Early on, he signed a long-term contract, which he wanted. He became the highest-paid shooting guard in the league. Within a year or so, he was unhappy about the deal. That sort of thing bothered me about Mitch.

Mitch was very unhappy about having to come to Sacramento in the first place, and at the end of his career with us, he'd become totally disenchanted with the franchise and had some real problems with the front office. He said some very personal things to people. His attitude hurt the franchise, and we didn't deserve that treatment from Mitch. That's why, quite honestly, I wouldn't have retired his jersey as quickly as we did. I think he deserved to be honored, no doubt, but I probably would have waited a few more years to make sure Mitch was truly aware of how valuable this franchise was to him. The reality was, "Well okay, you went to Washington, how did that work for you? You went to the Lakers, how did that work for you? And you were a major star where?"

We built the team around him, and we also built the coaching staff around him. Garry St. Jean was a guy Mitch really liked due to his association with the Warriors. There was never a day that Garry didn't bend one backward to try to make the team fit Mitch and make sure that Mitch was satisfied. That was a never-ending process. Getting Mitch was the best trade I ever made, but as terrific as he was as a player, some of the things he said and did were bogus.

Geoff continued to retool the team after the 1994-95 season. Spud Webb had given us about everything we could have asked; he definitely was on the downside when we sent him back to Atlanta for Tyrone Corbin, who became part of a later trade. We drafted Corliss Williamson, Tyus Edney, and Dejan Bodiroga of Yugoslavia. Dejan never played for us—he was a star in Europe and probably would have been mainly a role player here—but it showed that Geoff was ahead of the curve by looking at the global game for talent. European players ultimately would play a big role in taking us to the upper echelon of the league.

Mitch Richmond acknowledges the crowd. Rocky Widner/NBAE/Getty Images

Our first European was Sarunas Marciulionis, who we got from Seattle for Frank Brickowski. Frank was a good player, but he hadn't played for us because of injuries, so that was a no-brainer. Marciulionis had a lot of trouble with George Karl in Seattle. When we added "Rooney" with the group of guys we already had, we were about as physical as any team in the league. With Rooney and Mitch out there, there were many guards in the league who didn't want any part of us. Rooney could score, and that was the season they had a shorter three-point line for a while. That was exactly his range. The foot and a half or so made a difference for him. Rooney was excellent off the bench, fit perfectly into our style of play, and was a nasty one-on-one player.

After the All-Star Game, we finally got Billy Owens. We sent Walt Williams and Corbin to Miami for Owens and Kevin Gamble. I'm convinced that if Geoff hadn't made that trade we wouldn't have made the playoffs. Billy was in great shape and really helped us. We ended up winning 39 games again and reached the playoffs for the first time in 10 seasons. Mitch was Mitch, averaging 23 points, while Brian Grant, Owens, Olden Polynice, Rooney, and Tyus Edney all averaged double-figure scoring. Tyus—who was a star at UCLA—couldn't shoot, but he could get to the basket, and we had plenty of other facets working. Tyus is still playing in Europe and has made a significant amount of money over there.

We faced Seattle in the first round of the playoffs. Mitch gave us our first Sacramento-era playoff victory—90-81 in Game 2 at Seattle. He had a miraculous performance in that game. I think he scored around 35 points while defending Gary Payton. Although the Sonics had won 64 games, we felt confident after winning in Seattle. If Mitch hadn't sprained his ankle in Game Three … the series was closer than people realize. They were about to go to Choke City. We led most of the third game before Mitch got hurt, and they ended up winning that game and the next one to advance.

As good as the Sonics were that year, they ran into someone better in the Finals—losing to Chicago 4-2. The Bulls were at their absolute peak that season, winning a record 72 games. That was the best team I've ever seen, no question—mainly because of their defense. Now, they were a great offensive team. They should have been—they had Michael Jordan—but their defense was incredible. They didn't have much size; what they had were long, quick athletes. Pippen, Rodman, Jordan—all of them had long arms, quick feet, and great hands, and they found guys who fit there with them. They could just blot out teams.

That year, we played a preseason game against them. We were even or pretty close to even midway through the third quarter, then all of the sudden they decided to play. I mean, we couldn't even get off a *bad* shot. It was like, "Thank you guys for coming, now we're going to kick your butts."

That's how good they were—they just turned it up a notch and beat you comfortably. They knew that their three studs—Jordan, Pippen and Rodman—were going to be out there for 42 minutes a game. They ran the triple post/triangle offense, but at the end of the day, in the last six minutes of the game, it came down to Michael Jordan. They simply cleared the floor and got out of Michael's way.

They were better than Magic's Lakers, Bird's Celtics, or anyone else. The record would prove that, of course, but I think the Bulls were so special because Michael in his prime was the best defender in the world as well as being the best offensive player. We've never seen that before or since.

Despite our loss to Seattle in the playoffs, we thought that we had reached a turning point as a franchise. The situation was similar to the one after our first Sacramento season: If we kept the group together, we'd be consistent winners if not necessarily big winners. Mitch had a lot of mileage left, and we had some good young players. Going into the 1996-97 season, Geoff traded Rooney and a second-round pick that became Jeff McInnis for Mahmoud Abdul-Rauf, who had been a big-time scorer for Denver. Mitch had a great season, averaging 25.9 points, but Brian Grant missed much of the season, and Abdul-Rauf was a disappointment as a second scoring option. He was inconsistent, and it was obvious the best had passed for him. Beside that, he and Mitch didn't fit well together because they were both shoot-first guys.

We shipped out Rooney because, while there's no doubt he had helped us, his body was breaking down. Over the years, he had left a lot of skin—and maybe a few body parts—on the court because he was always hustling, diving, and scrapping for loose balls. We thought that Mahmoud might just need a change of scenery. He had been involved in some controversy in Denver because he refused to stand for the national anthem, but the consensus was that he had some good years left. The trade was one of those that didn't help either team.

We dropped down to 34 wins and missed the playoffs. That led to some frustration because everyone had been so optimistic. When things go wrong, the coach is the first guy in line to go. That's never fair, but that's the way it's always been. Eddie Jordan replaced Saint as coach in mid-March when we were 11 games under .500. We had won 40 percent of our games under Saint, which was a big improvement over Bill Russell or Dick Motta ... or me for that matter. Maybe it was just kind of time for Saint to move on. Some of the veteran guys had tuned him out. Saint and Mitch had a great relationship, but even that had worn thin. Saint was blamed for injuries and things that weren't his fault, but that's the NBA.

We didn't get any help from our first-round draft pick that season, but things turned out for the better because of that. We had used the 14th selection on a player we knew wouldn't be with us for a couple of years because of his contract with PAOK in Greece … Predrag Stojakovic. Peja was a very unpopular pick. The majority of our fans wanted John Wallace, who had led Syracuse to the Final Four. As the years pass, the people who were booing at the time would never admit it, because Peja is an all-star. The fans just *knew* John Wallace was going to be a star. Well, it didn't turn out that way.

No one in Sacramento had ever heard of Peja, and he wasn't going to join us right away. Maybe that hurt us in the short term, but overall, it was the best thing for us. Peja got more playing time over there than he would have here, so by the time he joined us, he was ready to play. Even then, he played behind Corliss Williamson for a while.

The difference between Peja and some of the European players who are coming into the league now is that Peja was a major star in Europe at 19 years old. Nowadays, the 19-year-olds from Europe who are coming in as lottery picks were reserves overseas who averaged six points a game. We take high school guys who often aren't prepared or mature enough to handle it, and now Euros are in the same boat. There was a time you could get Vlade Divac in the late first round or Peja in the middle of the first round. Those guys would now be top-five picks, because teams scout Europe almost as well as they do the NCAA. Even with Europeans, now we're looking at potential rather than for someone who's actually done something.

There was one other significant development that season: The Women's National Basketball Association and Sacramento Monarchs made their debut in 1997. David Stern and the NBA put the league together—there was an increasing awareness of the women's game, and NBA owners are always looking for ways to occupy their arenas in the summertime. We were one of the eight original teams. Geoff Petrie and I were on a committee to select the Monarchs' coach and general manager—Mary Murphy held both jobs—and at the time, that seemed to be the end of my involvement. We had enough problems with the Kings at the time.

Until midsummer, I'd watched a couple of Monarchs games and practices, but I really didn't follow them too closely. The team was sort of set up to fail, through no fault of its own. The league wanted the biggest stars in the biggest markets and didn't seem too concerned about the rosters of the teams in Sacramento or Utah— although it needed eight teams for scheduling purposes. Ruthie Bolton was our star, and she was a good player, no question, a first-team all-WNBA selection. However, compared to Lisa Leslie in Los Angeles or Sheryl Swoopes in Houston ... she wasn't the same caliber. There was a draft, but only after the league had placed designated players with each of the franchises. Rebecca Lobo went to New York, while Lady Hardmon was designated as the Utah Starzz' star. We were able to trade for her—she later became known as Lady Grooms—and she was a nice role player for us.

The Monarchs began okay before heading sideways. Jim Thomas became very frustrated with Mary and how she handled players. I don't know all the particulars, but it came to a head when the team was 5-10, and Jim wanted to make a change. I was in Utah with the Kings' summer league team when Jim called me and told me he wanted Mary out of both roles. He wanted me to take over as coach and GM. Of course, there wasn't any additional pay, so I wasn't very thrilled about it. I didn't want to do either job, honestly, but after talking to Jim, I came to the understanding that I probably ought to be willing to take one of the roles if I wanted to remain gainfully employed. Most people probably understand that sometimes you have to do things you don't want to do. So I agreed to become GM, and Heidi VanDerveer, who had been Mary's assistant, took over as interim head coach of the Monarchs.

I had no intention of enjoying it, and I admit I went into it with a totally bad attitude. But once I got into it, it became a challenge. The Monarchs were a really bad team, poorly put together. I was an expert on bad teams from my years with the Kings. Fortunately, there was no salary cap, so money didn't come into the picture in terms of fixing things. All we had to worry about was evaluating the talent and then upgrading it. Honestly, I was ahead of many of the GMs in the league. I knew how to make trades and was willing to work the phone lines to get them done. So I got involved and started learning the women's game and really came to like it a lot. I still do. It's basketball, and I have a tremendous amount of respect for the players. They're the best in the world.

I couldn't do much the rest of that first season because I was learning. The next season, I could start to try to turn the team around although we were still not good. In 1998, we had a great draft that started laying the foundation for the Monarchs to become a good team. We took Ticha Penicheiro, one of the WNBA's best point guards, with our first pick and forward Tangela Smith with our second. The following year we drafted Yolanda Griffith, our superstar, and Kedra Holland-Corn, another big-time player. We also hired Sonny Allen, who was an excellent coach and put in an exciting, open-court style for the 1999 season. But it was those four players who made the franchise and are still having an impact on it, because Kedra became Kara Lawson—I traded her my last season—and Tangela was traded for Nicole Powell.

I don't want to oversimplify, but the Monarchs have been one of the best teams in the league the last five years, and it's based on those two drafts more than anything else. We didn't make any egregious mistakes in the draft while I was there, and John Whisenant has done very well in heading up the Monarchs' last two drafts as GM and head coach. In that regard, the Monarchs have been perhaps the most effective of any of the WNBA teams.

I retired from the Monarchs in 2003. We went from being a bad team to a contender in a couple of years and stayed that way. I was proud of my role with the team. I made the first four trades in WNBA history, and I guess that would be my legacy from the women's game. They even hung a jersey in the rafters at Arco Arena with my name on it. While it's very nice, I certainly wouldn't have encouraged them to do that.

When the Kings played the Minnesota Timberwolves in the playoffs a couple of years ago, Flip Saunders came up to me and said, "Every time I look up there I see that jersey with your name on it. There's got to be a message or a moral there somewhere."

"Flip," I said. "There really isn't. I don't know what to tell you."

I also became involved in USA Basketball, helping to select the Olympic women's team players and coaches. That American team won a gold medal, by the way. I went from being a guy who wanted nothing to do with the women's game to truly enjoying playing a part in it.

The thing about the women's game that I admire the most is that the women have a harder road to become world-class players than the men. Very often, they don't get the same encouragement. Women really have to commit themselves, be more self-motivated, than their male counterparts, who often are pushed to be great players from the time they're very young. I enjoyed my time with them. I had so much fun sitting and talking basketball with Ticha or Yolanda or Ruthie, because they wanted to know more about the game, talk strategy and philosophy. They'd pay attention, ask you for advice, and actually take it. The NBA's not always that way. Some guys are good that way, but most aren't.

CHAPTER THIRTEEN

The Stars Were Aligned

Rumors abounded about the Kings moving out of Sacramento during the 1996-97 season even though the games were more or less still sellouts. The team asked for financial help from the city, and after a great deal of begging, pleading, and arm-twisting, we received a $70-million loan. Despite all the scrutiny the transaction received, no one mentioned the fact that Eli Broad, one of Jim Thomas's minority partners, probably had more cash in his sock drawer than the city had in its treasury. In any event, the loan averted a potential crisis.

I don't think we were close to leaving Sacramento, not that I necessarily would have known (Jim Thomas had come to trust me, but I wasn't part of his inner circle). There were reports that the Kings were going to Nashville because that city had just finished a new arena. Financially, things were not going well, and the owners were looking for a better deal. But leave Sacramento? That would have been a terrible mistake even though some of the fans were tiring of our lack of success. We wouldn't have done any better in Nashville, that's for sure; especially with the way we played during the 1997-98 season.

We've had more low points as a franchise than Michael Jordan had dunks. But that season, for me, was the worst and most disappointing year in my time with the Kings. Mitch held out in camp, missed a dozen games with injuries, and was going through his "I want to be traded" routine. Eddie Jordan had some real problems with Olden Polynice, as almost everybody did. Brian Grant signed with Portland as a free agent—although as it turned out, letting him go was probably one of the greatest moves the franchise ever made, crazy as that sounds. If he had signed the offer we'd made him, we wouldn't have had the cap room to make a much more significant move later.

But at the time, we just didn't have enough talent or desire. The team absolutely quit competing for Eddie Jordan at the end of the year and lost 19 of the last 20 games to finish 27-55. It was the most negative of times.

Although there had been grumbling before, that season was the first time the fans got absolutely sick of the team. I don't blame them—I did, too. There simply was nothing to be happy about. I can't think of a good thing about that year other than it ended. If things hadn't turned immediately around during the following season—which was the lockout year—who knows what would have happened? We went from having a reason to be enthusiastic again to a serious backslide.

Fortunately, for every door that closes, another one opens. One opened wide for us at exactly the right time, and good things were about to happen. There was a light at the end of the tunnel, and this time it wasn't a train. It was the Maloof family, which, in January 1998, bought a minority interest in the team. While they weren't running the show right away, it was clear that they would be soon. And even though there was no immediate impact on the team—we were still terrible—our mantra of "Wait until next year" actually had some meaning. The combination of the Maloofs' presence and the sense of urgency we'd developed led to some moves that completely turned things around in about a year.

Geoff understood—and to his credit, Jim Thomas prodded him—that we really needed to take some chances to put an exciting product on the floor. Geoff was ready to be more aggressive in signing players and making trades, and Jim essentially gave him carte blanche to do whatever he thought was necessary. We were going

Geoff Petrie (left) addresses the press as Gavin and Joe Maloof listen.
Rocky Widner/NBAE/Getty Images

nowhere as we were. When you lose 19 out of 20 to end a season, your risks aren't very great.

Actually, the first step toward redemption was a trade during the 1997-98 that didn't seem to mean much at the time. We sent Michael Smith and Bobby Hurley to Vancouver for Otis Thorpe and Chris Robinson. We had tried to give Bobby time to recover after his near-fatal traffic accident, but he never was any kind of a factor, and it was time for him to move on. Otis, who had been a stud for us early in the Sacramento era, was definitely close to the end. But he became a part of what probably was the biggest trade in franchise history when we sent him and Mitch Richmond to Washington for Chris Webber. A month after that, we finally signed Peja Stojakovic. Just over a week later, we drafted Jason Williams out of Florida.

As mama used to say down at the church hall, "B-I-N-G-O!"

There was more to come.

Geoff had done good things before, and he has since then, but that period was a marvelous point in time for the Kings. Everything came into place; every move was excellent. Generally, you make some mistakes and have some even-Steven types of things—but the stars were aligned. We deserved that, because there certainly were times when the stars were out of whack, and a black hole was enveloping us.

Strangely, the most important move—at least in the short term—was drafting Jason. J-Will was a risky pick based on his college career. Everyone knew that Jason was a bit of a flake (or a lot of a flake)—but this franchise needed Jason Williams. There were probably players better than Jason available, but there was no one who could have done more for us. Jason, more than anybody else, saved this franchise because he gave us a personality. He was the perfect guy for us at that point in time. We became a show overnight—from a team that no one wanted to see to the team everybody wanted to see.

When we talk about the glory years of the Kings, I'll always have a soft spot for J-Will. He was fun to watch, whether it was practice or in games. He was kind of like that line from *Forrest Gump*: "Life is like a box of chocolates—you never know what you're going to get." With J-Will, you never knew what was coming next. Lord knows what the future holds for him, because he's a young man who doesn't seem to understand himself.

I know that our division of basketball operations, Geoff, and I can thank him for the fact that we're still employed by this franchise.

Most people in Sacramento weren't familiar with J-Will when we drafted him. He came out of a small town in West Virginia that also produced Randy Moss—much like Larry Bird and I coming out of French Lick, Indiana. There must have been something in the water. Jason and Randy are both a little dingy—and a lot dingy as the case may be. He bounced around to three universities following Billy Donovan, who had originally recruited him.

We saw J-Will as a smaller version of Pete Maravich—not as good a scorer, but capable of doing more things with the ball. They were both equal parts erratic and spectacular. Jason can do things with the basketball that very few people in the history of the game could do. He is going to put on a show one way or another in the open court.

Jason Williams performs his "magic show." *Rocky Widner/NBAE/Getty Images*

When J-Will was at Florida, I saw him play a game against Kentucky in Lexington. Jason just destroyed them. Rick Pitino was coaching, and they had all the pressure defenses and all that, and Jason put on a show that took your breath away. Kentucky's defense didn't bother him at all, and even the Kentucky fans were applauding him by the end of the game. The next game, they played Vanderbilt or someone, and Jason committed 14 turnovers. But that was J-Will. His gifts—and his drawbacks—were obvious.

Like drafting Jason, trading for Chris took some guts. There was some concern about his reputation. He got into a power struggle with Don Nelson. He had some problems with marijuana. He had taken money (although no one knew how much at the time) while going to the University of Michigan. All that was a bit worrisome, but, again, this was a case where we needed to swing for the fences.

From where we sit now, the trade was a no-brainer. It didn't seem that way to people outside the organization at the time, though. There was a fair amount of criticism both in Sacramento and nationally. I remember one national columnist telling me, "You guys are asking for trouble. You're giving up Mitch Richmond—a great team guy, a star, a good guy in the community—for Chris Webber, who's nothing but trouble."

However, we knew there wasn't much risk. When you can trade a smaller guy for a bigger guy and an older guy for a younger guy, there's not much to worry about. We knew that Mitch was on the downside, and we had reason to believe that the best was ahead for Chris, which it was.

C-Webb was a good citizen and leader for us in addition to being the best player we ever had. Yes, there was the issue of what happened at the University of Michigan, but that had nothing to do with us. And, yeah, there were times when he came off as being too big-time to be in Sacramento when in truth we put him in the best possible position to succeed. All that stuff aside, up until his knee injury, Chris was one of the top 10 players in the league, and the Sacramento Kings had never had someone like that—including Mitch.

There was speculation—particularly from the East Coast media—that Chris would never play here. Of course, the East Coast media is almost never right about anything—from my experience.

C-Webb defines "dunkage." *Sam Forencich/NBAE/Getty Images*

I'm convinced some of those so-called experts never actually watch basketball games. Geoff, as usual, didn't panic. He stuck to his guns and said, "He's going to play here if he plans to keep playing." I think Chris held out for one day of camp, showed up at the urging of his father, and then things just clicked. Some of that was because of Chris's skill, and some of that was the guys we put around him. It was a tremendous fit for Chris, and he could see that. And he probably knew he needed to resurrect his career somewhat, which is exactly what he did. Thankfully, he resurrected us right along with him.

It was amazing that Geoff was able to pull off that trade. Washington panicked because of Chris's off-court problems, some of which were overblown and not even accurate. But looking back, Washington consistently did the wrong thing for years. They traded

Peja Stojakovic goes for three. *Sam Forencich/NBAE/Getty Images*

Rasheed Wallace for Rod Strickland. They traded C-Webb for Mitch Richmond. Ben Wallace was there for a while, and they let him go as a free agent. Juwan Howard was there. They really made some major mistakes, and that's why they were terrible for a time. Now they're back to being good. Eddie Jordan and Ernie Grunfeld have done a great job of rebuilding that franchise.

Mitch was tremendously valuable to this franchise both coming and going. He was our first major star, he helped the franchise get better, and gave us some credibility and something of a national identity. By trading him, we got a major star who took the franchise to a totally different level. Maybe I've become a bit jaded about Mitch over the years. Still, I appreciated him and respected everything he'd done for us. At the end of the day, we couldn't have asked for anything else from Mitch Richmond.

We drafted Peja Stojakovic in 1996, while he was playing for PAOK in the Greek Professional League. I'm sure many of our fans were convinced that we'd simply wasted a draft pick with Peja, but after he won the MVP award over there, he decided he was ready to try the NBA. So we ended up getting a great ball-handler in Jason, a superstar in Chris, and one of the world's greatest shooters in Peja in just over the span of a month. That's a pretty good month's work.

I remember looking out at the practice court from my office one time when Peja was out there by himself shooting threes—swish, swish, swish. I started counting. He made 42 three-pointers in a row. I saw it and couldn't believe it. As he was finishing up, a couple of our other players came out on the court. He told them what he'd done, and they didn't believe it. Peja noticed I was looking through the window and called me over. I said, "Yes, fellows, I saw it; and I was counting. It was 42 in a row."

Sometimes people take shots at Peja because they don't think he does anything other than shoot. Well, just find the next guy who can hit 42 threes in a row. I don't think any other human in the world has done that. I told Larry Bird that story, and he said, "If it wasn't Peja, I'd call you a liar."

CHAPTER FOURTEEN

Lockout—and Lookout

O n July 1, 1998, the NBA imposed a lockout that lasted 191 days. Generally, nobody wants a lockout. For us, however, the timing couldn't have been better. It gave us more of a chance to collect our thoughts and get our act together. During that time, we couldn't do anything involving players—no signings, no trades, not even any contact—but that didn't stop things from happening. The three big moves we had made to that point had been great, but they might not have worked out so well without the ones that followed—particularly the next one.

Eddie Jordan has proven to be an excellent coach, but with us, he was young and inexperienced; and let's face it, he had a bad team. It wasn't a good situation, and I should know. He was 33-64 with us when we let him go in August. A month later, Rick Adelman came aboard, and you have to give both Jim Thomas and Geoff Petrie credit: Rick was the right man for the job, especially with the group we had.

Rick had a great track record in Portland. He reached the finals twice, but like so many other coaches, he didn't have an antidote for Michael Jordan. Rick's time with Golden State didn't work out as well as expected, although the Warriors did far worse after he left, which I think is revealing. Rick was known as both a teacher and a coach who enabled his players to do the things they do best, so he was ideal to work with C-Webb, Jason, and the rest. I don't think anybody—Phil Jackson, Pat Riley, whoever—could have had more success with that group than Rick did. His patience was the big thing, letting guys play in a free-flowing offense, living with terrible turnovers and mistakes. If he hadn't had been that way, the Sacramento Kings would have been far less interesting to watch.

Before Rick joined us, the Sacramento-era Kings had never had a winning record. The franchise's last coach to go better than .500 was Cotton Fitzsimmons in 1982-83. I was still coaching at Rockhurst back then, and I'm pretty sure the Pony Express still stopped in Sacramento. We've had winning records all seven seasons Rick's been with us—five straight seasons of 50 or more wins—and he has more victories than any coach in franchise history ... even me. So, yeah ... it was a good hire.

Our basketball staff—Geoff, Wayne Cooper, Scotty Stirling and I—met constantly during the lockout even before Rick came aboard. When Rick and his lead assistant, John Wetzel, joined us, we had what you might call a plethora (I minored in English, believe it or not) of good basketball people—of collective knowledge, as much as any NBA front office, in my humble opinion. During that time, from October to January 7, 1999, when the lockout finally ended, we schemed, planned, and discussed all kinds of different scenarios. We knew that, once the lockout ended, there'd be a flurry of activity, and Geoff definitely had a blueprint in place.

On January 15, 1999, the Maloof family announced that it would become the majority owners effective the following July. That put us in the position to make some additional moves, big ones and small ones. Jim Thomas knew he wasn't going to on the hook for the long term, so it was full speed ahead. One week after the Maloofs' announcement, there was a red-letter day in Sacramento Kings history: We signed Vlade Divac, Jon Barry, and Vernon Maxwell, who were free agents; re-signed Corliss Williamson, our own free agent; and signed J-Will, our top draft pick.

There are only three ways to improve a team: through trades, free agency, and the draft. All those things hit in spades for us. We had major improvement through free agency; we had major improvement through the draft with Peja and J-Will, and major improvement through the trade for C-Webb as well. We also had some existing players, such as Corliss, who were improving.

Vlade was a huge signing. Had the franchise not lost Brian Grant to free agency two seasons earlier, we wouldn't have had the cap room to sign Vlade. If trading for C-Webb and drafting J-Will were shooting for the moon, signing Vlade Divac was like buying savings bonds: totally safe, totally painless, totally sensible. Of course, there were a couple of people around here—I won't say who they were—who argued that we should sign Ike Austin instead of Vlade. I'm thankful that one of those people wasn't Geoff Petrie. The majority of us certainly were in favor of Vlade. Geoff would have made his own decision, so I have no doubt how that would have played out. But at the time, there was concern that Vlade didn't show up every day, and Austin had a really good year in Miami before going to the Clippers and taking a step back. Even in the media, some "experts" wanted us to go after Ike Austin. None of them came back later to say, "We blew it."

Had the Maloofs not approved of signing Vlade, he may never have put on a Kings uniform. Jim Thomas wanted to get Vlade, but if he had to pay the entire contract, who knows if that would have happened? At the time, some fans and media were grumbling that we'd given Vlade too much money. Because we hadn't been a competitive team and weren't in a glamorous market, we kind of felt we had to be prepared to overpay a bit for top talent. As it turned out, if there's such a thing as getting your money's worth in the NBA, Vlade Divac was the best bargain this franchise ever made.

While Vlade had been somewhat erratic in his career, he also had been very productive at times. He was extremely consistent with us, and the style suited him. So as good as he'd been in L.A. and Charlotte—a major contributor on 50-win teams for the most part—he became the team leader in Sacramento and was what I call "the perfect teammate." In all my years in basketball, at every level, I've never seen a guy who was great with talented guys, great with not-so-talented guys, great in the locker room, and totally unselfish on and off the court. He was just the best, especially as a person.

Vlade Divac was the "perfect teammate." *Rocky Widner/NBAE/Getty Images*

On top of everything else, Vlade had a great sense of humor. A few years ago in Phoenix, I was out for an evening walk, and we were in a hotel a bit out of town. I was on my way back to the hotel, and I guess Vlade saw me coming, because he hid behind some bushes and jumped out at me. Talk about scared—I about soiled myself. Here's this hairy seven-foot-one, 270-pound guy coming at me out of the pitch black like he was going to strangle me. I about had the big one. My little heart was pumping Kool-Aid for about an hour after that. That was Vlade, the big goof. I love the guy, but I hope to have the opportunity to scare the hell out of him someday.

Speaking of Phoenix, the Suns could have had Vlade. They had been his first choice. But they chose Luc Longley instead, and we're eternally grateful for that. That probably helped send the Suns on a downward spiral for a while and allowed us to progress. Sometimes fate works for you rather than against you. Lord knows we had been on the wrong side of that equation many times.

Vernon Maxwell and Jon Barry were signed on a make-good basis, but they certainly impacted the team. Vernon wasn't playing much to start the season and about went bonkers. He was a bonkers kind of guy. He ended up averaging double figures for us, though, and he wasn't just a factor on the court: he did a great job of helping to keep J-Will in line. Jason really listened to him. Vernon was a Florida guy, for one thing, and he had been in and out of trouble during his career, so they had some things in common. Also, J-Will knew that Vernon would beat him up. I think there absolutely was some fear there, and Jason needed that to stay in line. Vernon certainly liked J-Will, but he knew J-Will was a younger version of himself and knew what he needed.

Jon, with his fire, showmanship, and all-around talent, was a big favorite with our fans. I always appreciated Jon because he was so bright. He was a bit like Danny Ainge in that he was not only a coach on the floor, but also sometimes off the floor and on the plane. That's not a knock, though, because sometimes the team needed that. There are people to this day who wish Jon Barry had never left the Kings. It's not a coincidence that where Jon goes, teams tend to get better. He's a role player, but he's a very, very good role player. He's sort of like Robert Horry in that respect. It took him a while to figure that out, but toward the end of his career, he's become more valuable than he was when he was young.

Our last major addition at the time was center/power forward Scot Pollard, who signed with us late in the first month of the season. He had been with the team a few games and hadn't played. We had some injuries, and Rick Adelman put him in against Utah. Scot battled the heck out of Karl Malone. I called Geoff Petrie that night and said, "Boss, I think we got one. This guy is fearless." When you play against Malone and get him cross-eyed, you're on the right track. We haven't had many guys who've been able to do that. Scot brought toughness and competitive spirit. He did the dirty work— little things like blocking people off the boards and setting screens. Our team didn't have enough of that then and still doesn't to this day. Scot was sort of like the guys who served Seattle well last season, Reggie Evans and Danny Fortson. You have to have stars, but you also have to have guys who allow them to be stars.

Scot was also a great example of where Rick sometimes doesn't get enough credit. Scot was a great fit with us but didn't do much before joining us and hasn't done much since. He certainly has had some injuries since going to Indiana, but he hasn't been nearly as productive as he was in our style and with our coaching staff. That happens with some guys who have been great with us: they often don't seem to be as effective when they go other places. It's sort of like the Jerry Sloan rule: You see guys playing well for the Jazz over the years, and they go elsewhere, never to be seen or heard of again. Not that this was the case with Scot, but sometime players get to thinking they're better than they are when it's actually the system they're in and the people they're playing with who make them better.

Because of the lockout, the season was shortened to 50 games. That may have worked in our favor. The way we played, every possession was either a turnover or a *SportsCenter* highlight waiting to happen. I don't know whether that would have been the best way to go for another 32 games. I'm pretty sure I would have lost all my hair. We won 10 of our last 11 games to finish 27-23 and make the playoffs.

No one gave us a chance in hell against Utah, which was at its peak. We took them to five games and had a great chance to beat them twice. John Stockton made a huge shot—like he so often did—to give the Jazz a 90-89 win in Game 4 at Arco Arena and send it back to Utah. In Game 5, Vlade had a little short hook to win the game. It was the shot he wanted and the shot that was drawn up in the huddle, but it came up a bit short. It was a great series. I'll never forget coming home after that game and seeing about 10,000 people at the airport waiting for us to arrive.

I knew then that good times were ahead, although it easily could have gone a different way. Had we missed the playoffs, I'm convinced that Geoff, I—and everyone in basketball operations—would no longer have been with the Kings. When the Maloofs initially bought into the team, there was no reason to assume that nine months later, when they officially took over, they'd want to keep anyone who was there. Instead, everything fell into place, the Maloofs were happy, and they kept the front office intact, as they should have. That's saying something.

The Maloofs took over an improving team and added another level. They have tremendous instincts for marketing, customer service, doing things in a first-class manner. The Kings became America's darling. Our games became more entertaining. There were celebrities in the stands and pregame festivities ... going to Arco Arena became more of a social occasion than just a game. It was the Maloofs' vision. Being casino owners and having been involved in the Houston Rockets some years before, they were able to hit the ground running. It was great to have a new ownership group that didn't require a transition period, a learning curve. That can be a painful process.

The NBA had—and may still have, for all I know—a rule that every team has to be on national TV once a year. That's how many times we were on for about 10 straight years. In the 1999-2000 season, it seemed like we were on about every game. We were sort of like the Phoenix Suns were the previous season—not nearly as good, but must-see TV. With J-Will, Vlade and Chris ... it all fit.

Our front office had been understaffed for years, and the Maloofs addressed that. But what really told me that they were big-

Gavin and Joe Maloof watch their victorious Kings.
Fernando Medina/NBAE/Getty Images

time was that we finally got a practice facility of our own, a 38,500-square-foot facility with offices, two basketball courts, and all kinds of physical fitness and therapy equipment that opened in 2000. I had been hearing for 15 years that was going to happen, and I was at the point where I'd have been happy with a big tent in the parking lot at Arco. Over the years, we'd practiced at the Highway Patrol Academy, American River College, Cosumnes River College, the Salvation Army, Natomas High School, and probably other places I've forgotten. When they started digging dirt on the practice site at Arco, I said, "Okay, these guys are the real deal." And they've certainly proven to be. It ain't bragging when you can do it, and they did it.

And we could do it on the floor, too.

CHAPTER FIFTEEN

Not Quite Ready for Primetime

The NBA is about top-flight basketball; almost as much, it's about top-flight marketing. Commissioner David Stern has talked about someday having an entire division in Europe—I hope we don't travel on one of those budget airlines that only serves peanuts—and the emergence of Yao Ming as an all-star has opened up a market of a billion-plus people in China. We began the 1999-2000 regular season with a road trip: two games against Minnesota in Japan. Maybe it was appropriate to have the NBA's rising force in the "Land of the Rising Sun."

We played before enthusiastic crowds of more than 30,000, splitting two games with Minnesota. The crowds were just as frenzied as they are at Arco, which is saying something. We had a six-day layoff after the trip to recover from jet lag, and then we went on a seven-game winning streak. We had some big-time aspirations. However, we closed out the season playing poorly, losing our last four games to settle for 44 wins. I thought we should have done better, but it was the most wins we'd ever had in Sacramento and the best record the franchise had since 1982-83, so no one was terribly upset.

We had made a couple of significant moves going into the season, letting Vernon Maxwell go and acquiring Nick Anderson to start at shooting guard. Nick had been an excellent player in Orlando and had a nice career. But when we got him for a future first-round pick and Tariq Abdul-Wahad, he definitely was on the downside and had a lot of injuries. He only shot 39 percent for us, and I'm not sure that he ever came inside the three-point line. He was a disappointment any way you slice it. A big part of the problem was that Nick was more of a small forward trying to play shooting guard. That deal was one of the few Geoff Petrie has made that wasn't a clear winner. Of course, Geoff, being a very smart man, did the smart thing and cut his losses sooner rather than later.

As for Maxwell, we knew that he was a short-term fix. The 50-game schedule the previous season was an advantage for us with Vernon, because he was a volatile guy in the long run. Vernon went to Philly for a short time, then Seattle. I talked with Larry Brown when the 76ers were getting ready to pick up Vernon. Larry wanted to know if he could still play, and I said, "Yeah, I think he can. But don't bring him in unless you have minutes for him, because he'll give you problems."

He wasn't going to be a happy camper if he wasn't playing. He'd be a disruptive camper, in fact. It turned out that Philly didn't have the minutes for Maxwell, and he became a problem. Yet, we got a good stretch out of him—another example of Geoff's ability to find just the right guy to fill a need.

We faced the Lakers in the 2000 playoffs, and although we lost the series in five games, we were on everyone's radar screens, and it was evident that the 50-win seasons were coming. C-Webb had a great series. While we didn't have any answers for Kobe Bryant and Shaquille O'Neal, Webber proved that he was an elite player, too, and the Lakers had no answers for him.

By that time, a generation of Kings fans had come to know me not as the former coach or general manager or the current player personnel director of the Kings, but as the color commentator on television broadcasts. When I'm in public, I probably get asked more about the telecasts and the commercials I used to do for Chuck Swift's car lots than anything about the team itself.

I did the Chuck Swift commercials for seven or eight years, and they weren't just on the Kings' broadcasts, but on every channel and on all the time. People remember them whether they liked them or not. I did many of those commercials over the years. I'm a very gifted performer.

Okay, I'm a ham.

In one commercial for the Dodge Shadow, I did a little song and dance—"Me, and my Sha-dow." No one will ever confuse me with Frank Sinatra or Tony Bennett, that's for sure. The worst one of all time was President's Day. They dressed me up as Abraham Lincoln and George Washington. That was not a high point in my advertising career.

When I first started coaching, I had a weekly program, *The Jerry Reynolds Show*. I'd talk about the team, have guests, and goof around. One time they introduced our dance squad—all these pretty young ladies showing their moves—and at the end, I came out and did a routine. That got some national attention, much to my chagrin. Of course, I was doing anything I could to draw attention away from what the team was doing on the court.

One of the shows worth remembering was during Pervis Ellison's rookie year. He hadn't actually started playing for us yet because he was hurt. We ended up spending all year waiting for him. He was supposed to be my featured guest, and he didn't show up. He skipped it. I remember thinking, "You know, this is not a good sign." I guess he was too busy in those secret practices or whatever. I saw him the next day, and he was as likable as he could be, apologetic, all that—but it was not atypical, as I came to find out. It was a good indicator of what was to come. Little things can tell you a lot about people.

These days, I fit my scouting duties around the television games, and we have about 70 telecasts a season. That schedule doesn't leave much time to look at college or CBA players. Being able to see NBA players play live and talk to more coaches, trainers, and media types than anyone else on our staff, I have a pretty good idea about the players who are in the league already. That comes in handy when we're thinking about making a trade or picking up a free agent.

I always liked doing television, but covering an entertaining, successful team is much more interesting. Broadcasts in the early

Grant Napear and I bring our viewers up to speed.
Courtesy of Maloof Sports & Entertainment, Sacramento Kings

years could lend to negativity, and let's face it: The Kings sign my paycheck, so while I try to be honest, I'm not totally objective.

Over the years, I've become more comfortable working with Grant Napear, our play-by-play guy. I think the world of Grant, I really do, but he's an acquired taste. I've told him that he's like coffee in that respect. It wasn't always the case, but now I have to have my coffee every morning, and I'm not sure I could work with anyone other than Grant. We're almost opposites. He's from New York, and I'm from the sticks. I'm pretty laid-back, and he's hyper. When we're on the team bus or plane, he's one of those guys who's always in a hurry. "When are we going to get there? This is taking forever." I just try to keep him from hyperventilating.

You've probably seen those television blooper shows, and I've had my share on Kings telecasts. One of the most embarrassing times for me, Grant, and the rest of the crew was during the 2002-03 season. Scot Pollard was hurt, and we invited him to be a guest commentator. He was going to come on the air in the third quarter. That game happened to be the one in which Jon Barry came back to

Sacramento with the Pistons. There was a story in the paper in which Vlade Divac told fans that they should boo Barry. It was a joke. As I mentioned before, Vlade had a good sense of humor. He knew that Jon had been very popular in Sacramento and thought it would be funny if the fans razzed him.

Scot and Jon were good friends, and Scot wasn't in on the joke. Apparently he was living under a rock; everyone else in the city knew what was going on. The fans booed Jon, but it was good-natured. They really respected and appreciated Jon for what he'd meant to us. Scot came on and went on a tirade against the fans who had booed. Then he threw his headset down and walked off, which certainly left Grant and me with egg on our faces.

I thought Scot was totally bogus. Not only didn't he get it, but he embarrassed us and made us look bad. He did to us what he thought the fans did to Jon Barry. He was all upset that people were being disrespectful to Jon and then was totally disrespectful to the television fans watching the games, who weren't booing Jon, and to Grant and me, who were trying to help keep Scot from sticking his foot in his mouth. It was a blunder. I've always felt that those things—bringing in a player or whatever during the broadcast—are almost always a mistake. I've told the powers that be as much.

Another gaffe I recall involved Jason Williams. The camera turned to J-Will, Peja, and Vlade sitting on the bench together. I made the comment—just an off-the-top-of-my-head line—that there were three people sitting together speaking a foreign language, and that J-Will might be speaking a language that nobody totally understood: West Virginian. As luck would have it, Jason's step-mother heard it, and she was totally offended. J-Will didn't have a problem with that comment; he got a kick out of it.

I was forced to apologize. I didn't see the reason. I'm country, and I know it. I thought the whole episode was stupid, and that it probably was a bad sign. If those were the people Jason was listening to, well, they just didn't get it. They were looking for problems. Good grief, being country's being country, and J-Will certainly was country. He was speaking West Virginian, for God's sake. His step-mother did, too. She just didn't know it!

As an NBA fan (not just because I'm on television), I watch many telecasts. The game I love—the announcers, not so much. On so many national games, there's so much talking going on that it's difficult for the viewers to get into the flow. On our telecasts, Grant and I have always tried to stay with the game and add bits and pieces during breaks in the play. I don't think there should ever be a time on a telecast where live action isn't shown. I don't like it when the sideline reporter on the national telecast is talking about what was said in the huddle or talking to some soap opera star in the stands while things are happening on the court.

I find the whole TBS show very tedious. So little is discussed basketball-wise that I feel it's not worth my while. When Magic's there, it picks up. He points out some legitimate things. But Kenny Smith and Charles Barkley just try to be witty and funny to a fault. Charles feels like he has to be outrageous all the time, and my question is, why should we care about Charles's opinion when he freely admits during the telecast that he really doesn't pay much attention to what's happening?

ESPN isn't any better. Steven A. Smith is out of control—he's trying to be the Dick Vitale of the pro game, I guess, just loud and obnoxious—and Greg Anthony and Tim Legler are, best as I can tell, experts on being experts. I can't believe that anybody except the people who hired them believe they have much credibility.

Bill Walton isn't very popular in Sacramento, but I actually enjoy him. He sometimes is too caught up in saying, "That play was horrrrrrrible!" instead of giving his insight. Still, I get a kick out of him because he'll end up arguing with himself. He'll make a point about something, and then go against it five minutes later, then go back the other way. People in Sacramento think he's against the Kings. I don't see that. He's going to be both for you and against you in the same game or the same series, and he's the same way for every team.

I like Bill Raftery, who does college games as well as pro. The real pros are the play-by-play guys. I've always felt that when the color analyst becomes the story as opposed to the play-by-play guy, you're out of whack. Dick Vitale talks way more on college games than the play-by-play guys, and I think it hurts the coverage. Doug Collins is really good. Hubie Brown is excellent, even though he pontificates sometimes. Of all the national guys, Mike Fratello might have been my favorite. He and Marv Albert worked well together, mixing humor and good information. Fratello didn't over-do it, and I knew he knew what he was talking about because he was a good coach. He was truly the czar. Of the younger guys, Steve Kerr has a chance to be good if he stays with it. He's knowledgeable, has a sense of humor, and doesn't seem too full of himself. I don't get tired of him as I do with some guys. Of course, he picked us tenth in the Western Conference last season. Well, everyone's wrong some-times.

I always tell people when I make public appearances that what I'm telling them is 80 percent crap and 20 percent pearls of wisdom, and it's their job to pick out the right 20 percent. The thing I try to avoid on television is overtalking. Grant and I try to focus on the game. You can't overanalyze or overdiscuss every play. A guy makes a 15-foot shot … how much more do you need to know?

"Ooh, that ball had great rotation on it. The score's 8-4."

Okay, let's move along.

CHAPTER SIXTEEN

Robert Roof

It may not have been the Summer of Love, but the summer of 2000 gave people many reasons to fall in love with the Sacramento Kings. Everything started to come together for us, as some shrewd front-office moves took us from a good team to a near-great one. We re-signed two key backups, Scot Pollard and Jon Barry, extended Peja Stojakovic's contract, drafted well, and signed two free agents who became major parts of a championship contender.

We made swingman Hedo Turkoglu of Turkey the 16th pick in the draft. You can imagine the excited reaction of 99.9 percent of our fans and the media: "Huh?" In that particular draft, everyone 18 and younger was the flavor of the day, so there were many older players available late. The guys we were focused on were Hedo, Quentin Richardson, Morris Peterson, and Desmond Mason. They were all available, and they are all far better than half of the guys who were taken in the lottery.

Hedo brought us versatility, a six-foot-nine player who had some point-guard skills and could defend shooting guards, small forwards, and some power forwards. Hedo is one of the guys who produces when he gets consistent minutes. He's not a guy who can come off the bench and light a fire, but instead a guy who fills up the stat sheet during the course of a game, not in bursts.

At times, there was debate about whether Peja or Hedo was the better player. There was a stretch during the 2000-01 season when Peja was hurt, Hedo averaged about 16 points and nine rebounds a game in his place, and we won all the games. Still, there shouldn't have been any debate. While we valued Hedo, Peja's the better player if for no other reason than he has an exceptional skill to hang his hat on—shooting. Hedo's a very nice all-around player, but there's nothing that truly outstanding about his game. Here's a secret: at the end of the day, in the NBA it's about putting the basketball in the hole.

While Hedo wasn't a fire-starter off the bench, we got one in Bobby Jackson. We had lost Tony Delk—who had been a valuable backup—to free agency. Our thinking was that Bobby might be as good as Tony. Within a short time, he was way, way better. Bobby had been good in Minnesota, but neither the Timberwolves nor we honestly realized how good he was going to be. When we got him he hadn't yet established himself as a three-point shooter, and to his credit, he has become a real threat. The guy is just pure heart and energy, and it's a shame he's had so many nagging injuries the last couple of seasons. Flip Saunders has told me several times that letting Bobby go was one of the worst mistakes Minnesota had ever made.

"I hope it is," I said. "Because if it's not, then you've really made some bad ones."

Bobby and our next big acquisition, Doug Christie, were alike in the sense that they had to bounce around a bit to get things figured out. Neither could find their niche; neither quite had the skills they needed, earlier in their careers—but we got them at just the right time.

We traded Corliss Williamson to Toronto for Doug just a month or so before the start of 2000-01 season. It was a trade of good player for good player; but it didn't help the Raptors, because they moved Corliss to Detroit, which was pretty silly. Corliss ended up winning the Sixth Man of the Year Award for the Pistons. He'd

Bobby Jackson is a fire-starter off the bench. *Rocky Widner/NBAE/Getty Images*

been great for us, and it still wasn't entirely clear whether he or Peja ultimately would be the better player. What was clear was that Peja had developed to the point where he deserved a lot of minutes. With his outside shooting ability, he opened the court up and gave our big guys more room to operate, which made them more effective. Corliss couldn't spread the floor that way, so trading Corliss was the right decision. Corliss was solid as a rock on and off the floor. It was a trade typical of Geoff Petrie in that the illusion of risk was just that: an illusion.

A long-armed, quick, six-foot-six great athlete on a team that didn't have much athleticism, Doug was a welcome addition. Nick Anderson had been the starter at two guard for much of the previous season, and I'll go on record as saying that Doug was better than Nick.

Doug could guard both point guards and shooting guards, which is something we needed. Earlier in his career, he had the reputation of considering himself a star-caliber player before he had really earned the title. That doesn't exactly make him unique, of course. Jerry West had him with the Lakers, and he told me that, while he liked Doug and thought he had lots of potential, Doug just didn't get it. Doug somewhat saw himself as Magic Johnson, Jr.—of course, we haven't seen that player yet.

When Doug was with Toronto, he finally started understanding what he was and how he could be most valuable. He's like many guys in that it just took him a while to get there. Most players come into the league thinking they'll be major stars—you don't get this far without a certain degree of cockiness—and they're not skilled enough. There are a few—the Magics, the Birds, the Jordans, the Amare Stoudemires ... it's a small group of natural-born stars. Doug was one of the ones who took a while. We got him at a time when he was coming into his own. Like Vlade Divac, Doug was a veteran who really got it. They were capable of star-type status, at least at times, but they didn't have to have it. They were both very comfortable fitting in and allowing the young guys to bask in the limelight.

Essentially, trading Corliss to get Doug not only improved us at both shooting guard and small forward but also made us more versatile. In turn, that made us a much better team, and we went from 44 to 55 victories, matching the franchise's best ever record. Peja justified our faith in him, averaging more than 20 points. He was runner-up to Tracy McGrady in the voting for Most Improved Player. We became an elite team by any standard and won a playoff series for the first time in the franchise's Sacramento era.

We lost the first game of a best-of-five series to Phoenix, and we caught grief from the critics. We shut them up by winning the next three. Peja takes a lot of crap about not coming up big in playoffs, but most of the credit for winning that series goes to him. By far, he was our best player in that series. Chris was off, and Peja scored 37 in the deciding game. For those who don't pay attention—which means most of the media, even in this area, and the people who call talk radio shows—Peja was the guy who came up big when most of our players (as well as our fans) wondered if we were capable of winning a playoff series. It was something we hadn't done before.

The second round was a different story. The Lakers swept us in four games, three of which were close. For us, it was a good wake-up call. We knew we were good, but we learned that we weren't quite good enough. Sometimes you have to find out the difference. We'd been too loose with the ball, among other things, and we didn't have enough experience. After that series, we knew that we still had some work to do.

Jason Williams had hit a plateau. Everyone knew what Jason was—tremendously talented, tremendously fun to watch, tremendously courageous, and sometimes erratic and maddening as all hell. He and Rick had struggled at times because J-Will wanted to play in the fourth quarter, but he didn't guard anyone, so Bobby Jackson was playing more in crunch time. That decision was a big part of our improvement, quite honestly. We'd won 55 games and wanted to get even better. We needed a more conservative player to become a serious contender, and we didn't see Jason as the guy to take us there. So the decision was made to trade J-Will and Nick Anderson to the Grizzlies for Mike Bibby and Brent Price.

The versatility of Doug Christie and Bobby Jackson allowed us to make the deal. We could play Bobby and Doug together a lot, so

Mike Bibby's ability to hit big shots makes him a great leader.
Rocky Widner/NBAE/Getty Images

even if the trade for Mike didn't turn out as well as it has, we were protected. J-Will's a point guard, so he needs the ball. If he doesn't have it, you don't need him on the floor. Bobby's a shooting guard offensively; Mike can play shooting guard offensively; and Doug can play point guard offensively, so the risk wasn't very great.

The Grizzlies wanted J-Will as much for his marquee value as for his play as a point guard, since they were soon to move to Memphis. The Grizzlies had become a little disappointed in Mike for reasons I'm not clear about. He came out of Arizona after his sophomore season and was the second pick in the 1998 draft. He was on the first-team all-rookie squad, averaged in double figures, and led the Grizzlies in assists. It's true the Grizzlies weren't very good, but it's hard to believe Mike was at fault.

I've always felt that point guard is the toughest position, and teams often give up on point guards too quickly—especially guys who come out of school early, whether it's Mike or Gary Payton or Chauncey Billups. Jerry West has told me that he's tried many times to find out exactly who made the trade with us. I guess nobody wants to take credit for it. Jerry would like to take a do-over on that one. Mike wouldn't have done for us what Jason did early—get a bored group of fans excited again—because he's not as flashy or exciting. But going forward, Mike Bibby was the guy who could make us a better team.

What we've learned about Mike over the last few years is that—in addition to being able to do exactly what we hoped he'd do in terms of giving us stability and consistency—he's also an outstanding clutch player. He wasn't involved in many big games or even close games with the Grizzlies, although he'd been a clutch guy in high school and college. Mike came here with the idea of fitting in. He stayed in the background the first year. He didn't want to step on any toes. As the year went on, he stepped forward, and he really emerged in the playoffs.

Every year, you see a little better player, which is what we hoped would happen. Mike's one of those guys who really likes to play and wants to be good, and it shows. He hasn't made the all-star team yet, but he probably should have, and I don't doubt that he will. He has some things he needs to do better—he's not exactly a stopper yet, but he's probably a better defender than J-Will—but he's one of the premier point guards in the league.

Shortly after we acquired Mike, we fooled the oddsmakers and our old buddies in the national media—those nattering nabobs of negativism—by re-signing C-Webb. Chris was coming off the best all-around season of his career. He had averaged 27 points and 11 rebounds and was named to the All-NBA first team—something no Kings player had done since "Tiny" Archibald in 1975-76. All season long we'd heard that Chris was going home to Detroit, or to New York, or to Timbuktu—anywhere but Sacramento.

Honestly, I don't think we were too worried about losing him. Prominent free agents—like Ray Allen last summer—typically go on tour so they can enjoy being courted, being wined and dined, being told that they're the key to winning a championship. Every city they go to, they say, "I've always dreamed of being a Cav or a Net or a Knick or a Heat. It's always been my deepest desire." Chris is the kind of guy who when he says it, he sounds like he means it. It was a distraction by the end of the year. I thought it affected him and his teammates, because there were so many questions everywhere we went. Here again, the East Coast media, bless their hearts, wrongly assumed that he would do anything to get away from the evil cow town of Sacramento that he absolutely hated.

I really get a kick out of some of the things that were said back then. For example, Chris supposedly disliked Sacramento because there weren't enough soul food restaurants in town. Generally, that's why you'd live in a gated community like Los Lagos with a bunch of other millionaires, 25 miles outside of downtown—to be near soul-food restaurants. I understand why players would want to live there: It's quiet, secluded, and secure. Eddie Murphy has a place out there. But, come on, you really can't say you miss the city and the sound of the streets and soul food restaurants when you choose to live that far out in the country. I know there are soul food places in certain parts of Sacramento, but I doubt they were places Chris ever thought about going.

There are many nice parts of Sacramento he could have lived if being in an urban setting was a big deal for him—Ronald Reagan lived in the Fabulous Forties near downtown—so my summation of it is, it really wasn't that important. One of Chris's strengths is that he communicates with everybody. One of Chris's weaknesses is that he tries to communicate with everybody. So sometimes he ends up telling people what they want to hear, which may seem polite but isn't necessarily the best thing to do.

With C-Webb under contract, all the pieces were in place for our greatest season—thus far. We started the 2001-02 season with Webber hurt, managed to go something like 15-5 until he came back, and didn't miss a beat when he returned. From just before Christmas until early February, we went 17-1. At the end of the season, with Peja hurt for 10-12 games, Hedo took his spot and played great.

It seemed like every time we had a bad game or a loss, we bounced back. We never lost more than two in a row. We were good on the road, winning nine of our last 10 and 25 all together. We were the deepest team and the most fun team to watch. You can back all that up with statistics—right there at the top in every category that counted.

Some of the experts said we weren't very good defensively, but our margin of victory was the best in the league, so I'm a little curious how we did that if we weren't any good defensively. We outscored our opponents by almost eight points a game. I guess some of our critics would have been happier if we'd held our opponents to 85 points a game and lost every game by three points. I guess that would have made us stronger. I always go by John Wooden's theory—he knows a little about basketball, I guess—if you want to know how strong a team is, margin of victory is what you look at. And we were the best in that category as well as in terms of record.

We won a franchise-record 61 games, making us the best team in the NBA—at least in the regular season. In the first two rounds of the playoffs, we blew through Utah and Dallas. The Jazz were a very physical, tough team. Some of the experts picked Dallas to beat us because they'd been very impressive in the first round. But we handled them in five games that were fun to watch. The key game for us was a 115-113 overtime win in Dallas in Game 4. Doug Christie came back from an ankle injury and put on one of the most courageous performances I've seen. That turned the series. I think we would have beaten them anyway, but it might have been a seven-game series. Doug just showed what he was made of and brought everyone along with him.

Then came the Lakers, the evil empire of the south. It's not hard to remember, just hard to talk about. We had a better record and a deeper team, but they had two players in Shaquille O'Neal and Kobe Bryant who were better than anyone we had, and that's a factor. It was a great series, which we expected, one of the highest-rated in recent times. It wasn't a tremendous upset, although it was tremendously upsetting to me.

People always discuss the shot that Robert Horry hit to win Game 4. If he misses, we're up 3-1 in the series and heading home. What all the brilliant experts in the national media fail to point out is that Horry—the Lakers' power forward, with his team down two points—was totally out of position on the play. Kobe drove and missed a shot to tie the game. Shaq missed the follow attempt, and Vlade Divac couldn't control the ball, so he tipped it toward the backcourt. Where's the Lakers' power forward? On the boards, like he should be? No—he's standing at the three-point line. People say it's sour grapes on my part, but it's not. It's absolutely a bad basketball play. There's no way that Phil Jackson expected or wanted Horry to be out there when the Lakers needed two points to tie the score at home and two shots already have been missed. They weren't worried about protecting the backcourt at that point. But Horry was there, and I give him credit: he made the shot.

That being said, we still should have won the series. Mike Bibby made a big shot to win Game 5 for us. Game 6 was in L.A.— the infamous 106-102 game in which many people thought the officiating might have been a little off. They won ... or they had more points at the end. The Lakers shot 27 free throws in that game and made 21. We shot nine free throws, making seven. Now, there's no reason a game should end up with both teams having the same number of free throws, but sometimes it's hard to understand the discrepancy. I've watched that game several times, as painful as it was, and it's hard to see some of the fouls that were called on us. I can't say that they weren't there, but anytime there could have been a foul called against us, it seemed like there was; and some fouls that could have gone in our favor weren't called. That's putting things in their best light.

When I'm doing public speaking engagements, people come up to me to this day and ask about Game 6. About all I can say is that, in my opinion, it was poorly officiated, and it worked against us. I don't think there's any doubt about that. We could have won the series there. I'm not saying the referees cheated, or the fix was in, or the league wanted the big-market team in the finals for TV ratings, as so many people have. All I'm saying is, just as teams have nights when they shoot poorly, officials have off nights.

We can't blame the officials or anyone else for what happened in the final game of the series. Unlike Game 6, we flat-out lost it. It came down to free throws on both sides. The Lakers were 27-of-33. We missed 14 of our 30 attempts in a game that Shaq made 11-of-15. When's Shaq going to do that again? Probably never—talk about the stars being aligned. I guess it was meant to be. If he makes his normal five of 12, we win. We weren't a great free throw-shooting team, but we were terrible that night—especially terrible down the stretch. You have to blame the players for that. There's no excuse for it. You just can't come up with one. Maybe it shouldn't have gotten to that point. But it was at home, it was Game 7, and we were the better team, in my opinion. Unfortunately, we didn't come up big, and Shaq—in particular—did.

Everybody knew that whoever moved on against the Nets would win the championship. If it had been us, we'd have been the champs. But I don't have a championship ring in a safety deposit box. To this day, I can't look at Robert Horry without thinking about the new roof I was going to put on the house with my share of the championship money. He cost me. I think of him as Robert Roof.

Our season ended in very disappointing fashion. Had we won the championship, I believe Rick Adelman would be viewed much differently. He'd get more slack from the national and local media, and we'd probably be in a new arena by now.

CHAPTER SEVENTEEN

Transition Game

Confession time: We flat-out should have won the NBA title in 2001-02. That being said, people have to understand how hard it is to win a championship or even to position a team to try to win one. Getting there is indescribably difficult, a combination of smart decisions by the front office, solid coaching, tremendous focus by the players, fortunate breaks, and probably a hundred other factors that are less obvious. That's why when you have a chance to win it; you have to go for it.

I don't think many of our players totally understood what it took because they'd never been there. I'd never been there. I think Rick Adelman knew what it meant to be at that point better than anyone did. Geoff Petrie understood—he was with Rick in Portland where they'd had some teams that had gone to the finals. You can't know what it's like until you experience it.

After the loss to the Lakers, probably all of us thought, "We'll get other opportunities." But we haven't—at least not yet. We had a great chance, but it didn't happen for us. Going back a few years, that's the difference between Houston and Utah. Utah was a better team for a longer period of time, but it was the Rockets that won two championships because they seized the opportunity when it was there.

Head coach Rick Adelman applauds his squad. *Otto Greule Jr./NBAE/Getty Images*

The experience we gained from being in the Western Conference finals would have played well in the 2002-03 season if things had gone a little differently. Our record wasn't quite as good (59-23), but we were a better team and probably better prepared to win the championship. As often seems to be the case with us, it came down to bad luck. And for those who don't believe in luck, let me tell you this: "Luck," like another four-letter word, happens.

Our 2002-03 team was one of the most talented and deepest the league has seen in a long time. Maybe C-Webb was our only superstar-type player, but I'm pretty sure that our second unit—Bobby Jackson, Hedo Turkoglu, Jim Jackson, Keon Clark, and Scot Pollard—could have been a playoff team in the Eastern Conference and a 40-plus-win team about any year. We had good players at every position and plenty of versatility. The toughest thing for Rick was trying to keep guys reasonably happy with enough minutes without affecting the main guys. We probably lost a few games just because it was hard to keep them motivated and interested. They were good enough that they knew if they just went out and played, they could beat anyone on any night.

Keon Clark signed with us in mid-August of 2002. He is a strange, strange character—right there with guys from the past like Jawann Oldham and Olden Polynice. He was in his own little world. On a very close-knit team, Keon went his own way. He wasn't disliked by anyone, but I don't know that he's exchanging Christmas cards with any of his former teammates either. I think Cleveland found out how different he is last season. Keon was a free agent, and the Cavaliers wanted to sign him. He failed to show up for the workout ... twice. Still, he was a talented guy who helped us win some games. He was athletic, could block shots, and play a little center and power forward. For 20 minutes a game, he was awful good. He could be a 40-minute guy at times, but I'm not sure you'd want a steady diet of that.

Jim Jackson joined us in December and proved to be a much better acquisition than Keon. He had been a big-time scorer earlier in his career who was a great role player for us—someone who could play smallish power forward, small forward, and big two guard. Jim took some minutes away from Hedo, which caused a little dissenstion with our fans. Jim had a reputation as something of a "locker-room lawyer," which explains why he'd never really stuck around in one place too long, but he made an effort to fit in with us.

That season we also had Damon Jones, who was a big contributor for Miami last year. We probably didn't totally appreciate what we had in him; that's been the story of his career. He's a bit like Jim Jackson in that he probably has talked himself off a team or two.

Bobby Jackson's presence was a huge factor in Damon's limited playing time. Bobby was at his best in 2002-03. Although he was hurt and only played 59 games, he was the first Kings player to win the league's Sixth Man of the Year Award—a well-deserved honor. Defensively, he was a little wild man. He guarded point guards and shooting guards and threw his body around inside to get tough defensive rebounds. There'd be a crowd of big guys scrambling for the ball, and Bobby somehow would come out of the pack with it to start a fast break. All his hard work came together that season. He shot 38 percent from beyond the arc and averaged 15 points, and while he and Mike Bibby are both small, Rick played them together quite a bit, and they created all kinds of problems for other teams.

It's probably best for the league that Bobby's only six feet tall and weighs just 185 pounds. If he had been born with Amare Stoudemire's body, it would just be plain unfair. He plays so much bigger than he is already, and he's fearless. I guess the Lord wisely doesn't let certain things happen.

Of course, it would have been nice if the Lord have given us a six-foot-10 Bobby Jackson in the playoffs that season. We beat Utah in the first round of the playoffs. Then came Dallas, which we'd beaten in five games the previous season. We took Game 1 easily in Dallas, but then Chris Webber suffered a knee injury in the third quarter of Game 2. Although we didn't realize it at the time, that was the end of that.

When C-Webb went down, it didn't seem that serious. I figured that he'd miss a game or two, then he'd come back, and we'd get them—Wrong. He ended up missing about the first 60 games the following season. Rather than just a scope, Chris needed major reconstructive surgery—what they call a "microfracture procedure."

Dallas beat us in overtime in Game 3, and we couldn't make up for that one. We were still capable of winning that series with a break or two, but we weren't a threat to win the championship once C-Webb was hurt. Looking back, what I find equally funny and unbelievable was that some people considered us chokers for losing to the Mavericks without C-Webb. What those folks didn't understand was the difference between C-Webb, a legitimate star, and the guys who replaced him. Hedo could play some power forward; Keon Clark could play some power forward—but they weren't Chris Webber, for goodness' sake. Chris was still Chris back then. He was our best player. Everybody on the team knew it, and everybody was comfortable with it. Most of the stuff he talked about then he could back up.

In basketball, people sometimes forget the obvious: Five guys play, and they're on both offense and defense. So every player is much more significant to the winning and losing of a game than they are in baseball or a football, just by the nature of the beast. And a star is even more of a factor. He has the ball more, he's on the floor more. Yes, you can make up for the absence of a major player for a short period of time—even in a playoff series—but you can't win a championship.

Would the Spurs, as good as they are, have won the championship last season without Tim Duncan? I think the answer is clearly, "No." That's the way it is, and many people missed that at the time. Chris was one of the 10 best players on the planet, and all the ninth and tenth men in the world can't make up for that loss. How many Devean Georges does it take to make up for the loss of a Kobe? There's no number you can name.

Following the loss to Dallas, we had to make a decision as a franchise: Were we still a championship contender as we were constructed or were we a team in transition, one that needed to make adjustments to remain a contender? We collectively decided—and I have no doubt it was the right decision—that Chris's injury marked a turning point.

Aside from Chris, our biggest concern was Vlade, who was starting to show his age—whatever that may be. As far as I know, no one knows exactly how old he is. An unsubstantiated rumor boasts that Vlade is the only guy in the league who's a member of both the

NBA Players Association and AARP. In July 2003, Geoff seized the opportunity to get Vlade's eventual successor. We acquired Brad Miller from Indiana as part of a three-way trade. The Pacers got Scot Pollard from us and Danny Ferry from San Antonio. The Spurs received Hedo Turkoglu from us, and Ron Mercer from Indiana.

Acquiring a high-caliber center, especially one who likes to play the way we do, is almost impossible. Brad could make shots from the elbow and find cutters—the two key skills we needed from a high-post center. Even though Brad was an all-star, he probably has turned out to be better than we anticipated. While he's not the kind of guy who generally can take over a game by himself, he's capable of that on some nights. Where he really excels, though, is being a key part of a system that works.

The trade for Brad points out something important about Geoff Petrie as a general manager. Geoff's a very sentimental guy—very appreciative of the players who helped turned this franchise around. At the same time, he's the consummate businessman—not at all sentimental. He understands that things are always in transition in the NBA, and one has to be prepared.

I remember the scene some years back when Rick Pitino was struggling with the Celtics. He told the Boston media that Bird, McHale, and Parrish weren't going to walk through the locker room door and suit up. The fans still wanted that—they were still living in the glory days. But Pitino was absolutely right. In fact, Bird, McHale and Parrish probably were allowed to walk through that door too long. They all got too old at the same time, and the Celtics went from being a great franchise to falling off the map when those guys retired. The Celtics still haven't fully recovered—partially due to Len Bias's death, of course, but mainly because they didn't know when to say goodbye. Boston wouldn't have traded Bird, but the Celtics should have considered trading McHale or Parrish and getting some major young players back. Like Branch Rickey used to say with the Brooklyn Dodgers, "It's better to get rid of a guy a year too early than a year too late." Sometimes you regret doing that for a season, but then you move on.

C-Webb missed most of the 2003-04 season, and Rick Adelman was forced to improvise. We had traded Keon Clark short-

Geoff Petrie introduces Brad Miller to Sacramento. *Steve Yeater/NBAE/Getty Images*

ly after the Miller deal, and our only other power forwards were journeyman Tony Massenburg and Darius Songaila, who has proven to be a valuable player but was an unknown commodity at the time. So Rick put both Vlade and Brad in the lineup, and it worked like a charm. We had the best record in the league for two-thirds of the season. Brad adjusted very well and showed that he could play either power forward next to Vlade or center when Vlade was out of the game. Brad was very unselfish and willing to do whatever needed to be done. Peja became more of the focal point on offense and finished second in the league in scoring at 24 points per game. Mike Bibby and Doug Christie also had great seasons.

We were playing very well, but it's also true—and this part has been forgotten—that we were very much aware that the early part of the schedule was the easiest part, and things would get harder as the year went on. C-Webb came back just as the schedule was getting tougher, and we were under .500 in the 23 games he played. Rick took heat for putting Chris back into the lineup and bringing Brad off the bench. Rick's thinking was: as well as the team was playing, it didn't have a chance to win a championship without Chris playing at a high level. I can't argue with that logic.

The team would have struggled down the stretch regardless of whether Chris was playing. The fact was, Chris came back, and the adjustment wasn't as smooth as we'd hoped. C-Webb had moments when he was very good and moments when he wasn't. The team lost some continuity after his return. Rick was in a Catch-22 situation. It's always easy to go back and say, "Chris should have come off the bench." However, if Rick had done that, and the team had finished the same way or worse, he certainly would have been criticized. People would have said, "Why didn't you play your best player? Why didn't you get him ready for the playoffs?" No matter what Rick decided, he simply was going to be wrong in part of the fans' eyes.

We finished 55-27, and by the time we got to the playoffs, C-Webb was playing well. We beat Dallas in the opening round and then faced Minnesota. By that time, C-Webb probably was back to being our best player again. Unfortunately, other guys were experiencing some slippage in their play. We lost to the Timberwolves in seven games. C-Webb just missed a three-pointer to send Game 7 into overtime.

If we'd have won that series, everyone would have been ecstatic. Despite the loss to Minnesota, our mood was upbeat at the end of the 2003-04 season, although it looked as if we'd drained every drop out of Vlade. He had given us everything he had—not that he can't still play, but now he's a limited role player rather than a main guy.

We asked ourselves, "Can this team get better?"

The answer was, "Yes, but it's going to be a little different."

The way C-Webb played against the Wolves, we had reason to believe that he might be able to get back to his pre-injury level with a summer of rehabilitation. And if Chris could have done that, we were confident that our starting frontcourt—C-Webb, Peja and Brad—could compete with the best in the league. There was no reason to believe Mike Bibby wouldn't improve. While Doug clearly was past his prime, we thought he was capable of another big-time season.

Letting Vlade go as a free agent was terribly difficult. Beside the fact that he'd been such a good player and had played such a big part in turning the franchise around, there was nobody connected with the team who didn't think the world of him. One didn't belong in this league if he didn't like playing with Vlade.

From our perspective, it was fortunate that the Lakers made an offer that Vlade couldn't turn down—one we didn't feel comfortable matching. We certainly had too much respect and appreciation for Vlade to kick him out on the street, but the fact that it was a good deal for him made it easier for us to let him walk away. The situation couldn't have worked out better: Vlade had a home in Los Angeles. He was part of the Lakers' legacy and—not to seem mean-spirited—we didn't feel like he'd come back to haunt us.

So we entered last season hoping for another title run without one of our cornerstones and at the same time wondering whether a major reconstruction project might be on the not-too-distant horizon.

Mike Bibby and Peja Stojakovic break down the defense.
Otto Greule Jr./NBAE/Getty Images

CHAPTER EIGHTEEN

Long Live the Kings

When you make major roster changes, you cross your fingers and hope that everything works for the best. Our only hope to remain an elite team last season was for everything to break just right. Unfortunately, it didn't take long to realize that C-Webb wasn't back to 100 percent and might never be, and while Doug still gave exceptional effort, the mileage was taking its toll. We were winning games, but not quite as easily. We didn't have the same depth. We were still a good team, but not a legitimate contender.

From a personal standpoint, it's very difficult to make the decision that it's time to shake up the team. You grow to like players and care about them. You know your fans have an attachment—particularly in Sacramento. And, while it's sometimes forgotten, players are people, too. They like to know they're valued by a team, and a trade can mess with their lives and psyches. Pro basketball is a business, true, but there's a relatively small group involved—front office, coaches, and players—and we're all in it together. So you don't make big trades lightly.

That being said, we'd already gone through the gut-wrenching process of parting with Vlade, and that helped steel us to make the next logical moves. The trick for Geoff Petrie was to make deals that

Doug Christie soars to the rack. *Rocky Widner/NBAE/Getty Images*

allowed us to move forward while continuing to win. The trick for Rick Adelman, which was even more difficult, was to integrate new players into an unfamiliar system while maintaining that high level of play. From a coaching standpoint, it's extremely difficult to have the team churned up—to lose guys who have been key players on big-time winners and not to have much of a fall-off. Rick never received the credit he deserved for winning 50 games last year with a squad that not only changed personnel and styles, but also had major injuries.

We sent Doug Christie to Orlando on January 10, 2005, for shooting guard Cuttino Mobley and forward Michael Bradley. Geoff saw the opportunity to get a younger player with a smaller contract. Cuttino came in and helped us win a couple of games right off the bat, which allowed our players and fans to accept him more readily than they otherwise might have. He's a very different kind of player than Doug—more offensive-oriented. There were times when Cuttino didn't look like the ideal fit for us, but at the same time, he was on the court. Doug only played 21 games for Orlando before shutting it down for the season.

There was a rumor making the rounds that we traded Doug in part because he was a bit eccentric. People made a big deal about his hand signals to his wife, Jackie, during games and how they supposedly were talking to television people about doing a reality show. The trade was made strictly for basketball and financial reasons: Doug was an older player who had lost a step and is due $8 million this season. We'd become accustomed to Doug's somewhat different ways, and everyone on the team liked him. If he wasn't such a self-less teammate, maybe you'd have heard some grumblings, but no one ever put him down. As for the reality show, there are only 18 billion of them on these days, so who cares?

If Chris Webber had snapped back into form and Bobby Jackson had been healthy, would we have made the Christie trade? I'd guess no, because we'd have probably felt we could make a run at the championship. But once we all agreed that we probably weren't going to need to have our ring fingers measured, we decided to try to rebuild on the fly—get younger, deeper, and better prepared to win in the future without taking a major step backwards.

With that in mind—going back to the end of the 2003-04 season—Rick couldn't have handled things any better than he did. If he had done things differently at any step of the way, we wouldn't have been able to trade Chris. If Rick had used C-Webb as a reserve or limited his minutes as a starter—not allowing him to put up the numbers he did—C-Webb wouldn't be in Philadelphia today. We'd still have a Chris Webber who isn't quite Chris Webber anymore at $20 million per season.

When you're paying anybody—Shaq, Kobe, Tracy McGrady, Tim Duncan, whoever—a superstar salary, one that takes up 30 or 40 percent of your salary cap, you have to have a major star. If you feel that that's changed, that the player isn't a star anymore, you have to do something. We've never had a player of Chris's caliber, and who knows when or if we'll have one again? He was the key guy to all the success we had. At the same time, if he got hurt again or couldn't bounce back to an all-star level, we'd be in deep trouble—totally hamstrung under the salary cap rules.

From our viewpoint, Chris, for all his contributions, couldn't play at the same level going forward, and we needed to get out from under that contract and bring in some players. Chris didn't have the lift or lateral movement he once had. Before the knee injury, C-Webb was one of those magnificent athletes who could run easily, was a quick and strong jumper, and could go through guys around the basket.

Some people were surprised that we'd trade C-Webb, or trade him when we did. Others were surprised that we *could* trade him. Most of the national media thought it was a home run for Philly. They saw C-Webb as he used to be and asked, "Why would the Kings trade one of the five or six best players in the world?" Well, the Kings wouldn't have, and didn't. Geoff Petrie had been looking into making the deal for some time, but quite honestly, there weren't many potential trades out there for a guy with bad wheels and a huge contract. We weren't mulling over 17 offers. Geoff made the best deal he could. Most basketball people saw that Chris was damaged goods.

Maybe C-Webb can, by some miracle, get back to that superstar status in the future. I'm rooting for him. But none of the guys who have had the kind of knee microfracture surgery that Chris had—Penny Hardaway, Allan Houston, whomever—have come all the way back. Chris has come back better than any of those guys, and he's still a good player. That's where some of the Webber-haters have been unfair: He has worked hard and deserves credit. Chris has adapted his game. He's made himself into a better shooter—almost to a fault. He sometimes settles for the outside shot because it's harder for him to go inside. I'm not putting him down: Larry Bird did the same thing after he started getting injured. Larry started taking more 20 footers because they were the best shot he could get. Chris was still getting his 20 points, but he was taking more shots—and from longer range—to get them. Three years ago, he'd get 22 points and 11 rebounds in his sleep.

Although C-Webb's final exit was not as positive, his place in Kings history is. *Rocky Widner/NBAE/Getty Images*

Things change due to age, injuries, whatever. Probably the best example is Michael Jordan coming back the second time. Michael was still really good, but he wasn't the best player in the world by any stretch. The game was harder for him. He still cared, and he still wanted to be the best in the world; he just couldn't be. Paul Newman's still a great actor, but he can't play Cool Hand Luke anymore. He can't be a leading man anymore. Can C-Webb? Time will tell.

Chris's evolution from inside to outside player was a big factor for us, because we really didn't have another low-post threat. We hoped that Chris could come back and establish that for us, but he just didn't have the legs under him and couldn't do it consistently. We've seen that many times with big guys who are injured.

In exchange for Chris, we got three guys—Brian Skinner, Kenny Thomas, and Corliss Williamson—who are players. Whether we keep them all or not, they all have value around the league. We have more flexibility as well as the chance to win just as many games by playing a little differently. If the Philly deal hadn't gone through, there might not have been a trade, period.

Much was made of the dynamic between Peja and Chris. Without naming names, C-Webb criticized some of his teammates after the Minnesota series, and many people assumed that Peja was his main target. So what if Peja was the target? A guy was disappointed in losing and popped off—happens all the time. The media wanted to make it out as if there was a Peja clique and a Webber clique in the locker room, portraying it as an either/or situation. That simply wasn't the case.

Peja and Chris always liked each other. Chris's game didn't fit Peja's as well as Vlade's did, and I'm not sure exactly what you do about that. I thought, at the start of last season, that Chris went out of his way to find Peja. Because he's not a one-on-one guy, Peja needs guys to find him, and Vlade was good at that. Chris was, too, although he might not have found Peja as often as Vlade. That wasn't a matter of dislike, though. People have a tendency to attach personalities to it when it's really about the way guys play.

The difference between Vlade and Chris was that Vlade really did look to make the pass first. That was his instinct. Whether he was playing with Magic Johnson or Larry Johnson or Peja, Vlade was a facilitator. While Chris is a very good passer, his first instinct is to score. He is used to being the guy the team looks for, with good reason. That's probably why he had some problems with Allen Iverson last year. Now, Chris probably needs to make some changes because he can't do some of the things he once could, plus he doesn't have the ball in his hands, and it's not going to be there nearly as often.

Essentially, what Geoff did with the C-Webb trade was take a big contract and break it into smaller pieces. We certainly don't have any problem keeping any or all of the three guys we got—perhaps in different roles than they had at the end of last season—and all three are tradable. Kenny Thomas has been a double-double guy—a starter on some good teams. Corliss Williamson was the Sixth Man of the Year a couple of seasons ago. Brian Skinner was a starting center in Milwaukee on a playoff team. The guys we got aren't major stars, but they're also not chopped liver.

After the C-Webb trade, we won two straight road games, beating the 76ers in C-Webb's Philly debut and then a good Washington team. But faster than you can say "delusions of grandeur," fate once again kicked us in the shins. Brad Miller broke his leg at the end of the Washington game. We already were without Bobby Jackson, who was recovering from a torn ligament in his left wrist. The combination of remaking the team and playing without two major guys down the stretch was asking a lot. We gimped into the playoffs with a 14-11 record after Brad's injury. At least we managed to win 50 games for the fifth straight season.

Brad came back for the first round of the playoffs against Seattle, but he wasn't the same guy coming off a broken leg. Not many players would even have tried to come back that quickly. Brad was able to play pretty close to normal on offense, but he wasn't close when it came to defense and rebounding. He wasn't able to react as well, which is perfectly understandable. Defensively, you're reacting to the other guy. Rebounding, you're reacting to the ball. Offensively, you can kind of plan things out and control things more, so Brad could be more effective that way.

The Sonics took us out in five games, which, given the circumstances, shouldn't have come as a total shock. For those out there who have questioned Peja Stojakovic's toughness in the playoffs, it should be noted that he led us in scoring in three of the games, including 38 points in the last one. If, like some of the talk show hosts seem to think, anything less than a championship is a failure, I guess we failed. Of course, by that standard, it's very difficult to be a success. If that's the only gauge, then any talk show host who doesn't have the highest-rated show in America is a failure, too, right?

When we first became good, our only goal was to continue to be good. Nowadays, a 50-win season can be a disappointment. I guess that's a compliment, in a way. If we'd have only won 49 this year, people might have come to Arco Arena with tar and feathers. That's fair; it's the way it is. But look what happened last season with the Lakers and Timberwolves, the two Western Conference finalists from 2003-2004: Neither team made the playoffs. There's nothing unusual about a significant drop-off when things change. Fortunately, it didn't happen to us. That in itself is significant, and it bodes well for the future.

Without having a healthy Brad at the end of last year, it's hard to say exactly how it all fits together. We saw good things from Kenny Thomas. Brian Skinner gave us some athleticism and shot-blocking. Darius Songaila continues to improve. We know Bobby Jackson can play if he gets healthy. In my mind, though, Brad is the key. He's the guy who can be Vlade II. As we move into the next incarnation of the Kings, Brad can be the facilitator who makes things work smoother for everybody. That has to happen if we're going to continue to play our style and be one of the premier offensive teams.

We have three guys who are all-star caliber: Brad, Peja, and Mike Bibby. I have no doubt they'll be terrific together. The challenge is to bring in the right pieces to make the team work without a Vlade, Chris, or Doug Christie. The three main ways to get better are the draft, trades, and free agency, and all those things are available, just as when the team originally took off. We were pleasantly surprised to get Francisco Garcia with the 23rd pick in the draft. Some of the media wags seemed to think that he's the same type of player as Kevin Martin, our first-round pick the previous season.

We're hoping that Kevin can ultimately be a bit like Rip Hamilton and ultimately Francisco can be more like Doug Christie. We may not be able to get a big-time free agent because of the money situation, but you can get help with guys who aren't stars like we did years ago with a Jon Barry or Vernon Maxwell. As for trades, who knows what's going on right now in the wonderful and mysterious mind of Geoff Petrie?

Getting back to that championship-contender status will be difficult. The good news is that our ownership group, our front-office staff, and our coaches don't need directions on how to get there. With the nucleus we have now, it will be easier to get back to the top than it was to get there in the first place as a lottery team. We haven't won a championship, but we sure know what it looks like and how difficult it is to attain.

Skill is a part of it, but like in so many things, that four-letter word, "luck," always plays a role. We've had some bad breaks lately. The major injury to C-Webb, in and of itself, was enough to impact this franchise dramatically. Had he stayed healthy, who knows what would have happened? Maybe a championship, maybe not. In any given season, there are four or five teams capable of winning the title, and for several seasons, we were one of them. Last year we weren't—but we're not starting from the bottom. We're not in a bad position. The prevailing feeling here is optimism—realistic optimism.

Every team has expectations each season. There are always a couple of teams that come out of nowhere and overachieve. Look at the Phoenix Suns last year: Who thought that they'd win 62 games? Nobody, that's who. This season, if they win 56, there will be people who are disappointed. Unfair, but true. Seattle last season won 50-something games when nobody thought they'd make the playoffs. There are also underachieving teams. Last season, the Lakers and Timberwolves were great examples. Most people thought the Utah Jazz would be much better than they were. I certainly hope that we're going to be the overachievers.

Our fans have every reason to be optimistic—as long as they're realistic.

Epilogue

Has it been 20 years since I followed the Kings from the Midwest to Sacramento? Sometimes it seems like it's flown by, sometimes it seems like it's been 120 years. I never came here with any thoughts of being here this long, so it's overwhelming to contemplate. I always kind of went year to year, hoping I could survive in some fashion and trying to do whatever job I was given well enough so they'd want me back—either in that job or another one. To be in one place so long, especially in the NBA, and especially after not having much success with the franchise early. ... Well, I'd have lost the ranch on that bet.

I've always felt that if I have a strength or ability, I'm willing to try to make myself valuable some way or another. If that meant doing more speaking engagements, or being available for a team or community function, or being an assistant coach, or being in the front office, or doing radio or TV, or working with the Monarchs, I tried to make the best of it. I've taken on whatever job needed to be done—not always with the best attitude, but always with good effort—and that's allowed me to stay here.

I'm glad, because I truly wanted to stay. If I have a goal in the league, it's to retire here in the next three or four years. If I had my druthers, I'd like to work one year in a new arena before I go off to the big arena in the sky later on—much later on. Of course, I wouldn't turn down a championship ring, either.

Building a new arena for the Kings is a big controversy in Sacramento these days, and I just don't understand it. The sports public in town has been somewhat spoiled. Gregg Lukenbill brought the Kings to Sacramento when none of the local politicians was willing to help him. He built two arenas with no taxpayer dollars and had to fight city hall every step of the way. When the Kings became huge, everyone wanted to step in and take credit.

I'm disappointed that the city and the region haven't learned their lesson. I'm a taxpayer, and I don't want to pay for everything, either. But I do understand that we need a new arena at some point, and those of us who want to use it—not just Kings fans, but anyone who wants to go to a big-time concert or car show or whatever— should be willing to pay something. There's a certain percentage of people in every city who are against everything. Their attitude is, "Someone's for it, so I'm going to be against it." That seems to be happening now as there's talk of a new arena. I hope we get past that.

Young people have asked me, "How do I get a job in the NBA?" and I'm quite honest with them: I don't know. That was never my goal. My goal was to be a schoolteacher and maybe a coach. If I'd have stayed at Rockhurst College, I'd have been happy. I could have been coaching there right now and probably—not meaning to be immodest—have one of the best records in small-college history. I'd be like Crash Davis in *Bull Durham,* the guy who held the unheard-of minor league home run record. On the other hand, he ended up with Susan Sarandon, which isn't too bad.

So often people look at the NBA and place more value upon it than they should. I don't feel any more important or valuable doing what I'm doing now than I did when I was a small college coach. Actually, I probably was doing more for humanity then. I make a better salary now, for which I'm very thankful. And being with the Kings has allowed me to work with so many interesting, wonderful people. I get to watch a great basketball team; the fans are great; we travel on chartered jets and stay in the nicest hotels; we get a per diem. What a deal! You can't beat it with a stick.

There were times back in the bad old days when I thought I'd end up coaching tennis or being the athletic director at some small college in California. If that had happened, I'd have made it work. I believe that it's about making yourself happy—take whatever situation you have and make the best of it. Of course, I'd probably have a difficult adjustment if I suddenly had to put up hay for a living, I must admit. I'm not sure I could kid myself into thinking I was happy about that.

Looking back, I've been fortunate in that I've never had a bad job. Truthfully, perhaps being a NBA head coach was the worst one. I knew I wasn't ready. I did the best I could, didn't do too well, and didn't coach again. But because I didn't really want that job in the first place, it didn't consume me. I never really pursued anything in the NBA, just took what came my way. Some guys are like Captain Ahab—always chasing the white whale.

I never chased the whale. He's chased me a few times, but he hasn't caught me yet.